TABLE OF CONTENTS

iv **Preface**

vi **Acknowledgments**

viii **Introduction**

SYMPOSIUM TRANSCRIPT

1 **Keynote Address on Liberty and Virtue:
The Case for Rebuilding Civil Society**

17 **Debate: Building a Coalition to Relimit Government
and Rebuild Civil Society**

39 **Panel Discussion: Designing Legislative Measures
to Strengthen Civil Institutions**

64 **Luncheon Address:
Charitable Efforts to Replace the Welfare State**

81 **Private Sector Community Development:
Creating the Means**

   81 Model Programs: Presentation of Samaritan Awards

   95 Committed Individuals

   102 Bridge Organizations

114 **Panel Discussion: Launching a New Social Movement**

141 APPENDIX I

The Greatest of These is Love
A Faith-based Alternative to the Welfare State

164 APPENDIX II

The Last Word
My Favorite Volunteer

PREFACE

In December of 1995, on the eve of the national debate over welfare reform that culminated in Congress passing the 1996 welfare reform act—and President Clinton signing that act under intense electoral pressure—the Family Research Council convened the conference now preserved in these pages. We did it out of a special sense of our responsibility, as leaders of the social conservative movement, to articulate a positive vision of a future that is profoundly compassionate even as it is radically non-statist.

Economic conservatives have analyzed the empirical failings of the welfare system; libertarian intellectuals have articulated a moral critique of state-enforced redistribution, but until recently, most critics of the welfare state have implicitly assumed that a sustained look at the question "What would happen if welfare weren't there?" would make their position increasingly unsalable, if not untenable.

That is why this conference, and the theorists and practitioners whom it brought together, are so important. We are beginning to see that the welfare state is not a bandage that must be kept on while the wound heals: it is an analgesic poison, temporarily assuaging the pain of the wound while actually preventing healing, and indeed spreading the wound further.

Alleviation of poverty is an intensely personal goal, yet welfare makes it the work of government-salaried professionals.

Alleviation of poverty requires roots in the communities of the poor, yet welfare consists of mandates from distant capitals based on theories from even more distant faculty lounges.

Alleviation of poverty requires an appeal to the best within each impoverished person, yet welfare encourages the worst.

Alleviation of poverty requires respect for the dignity of each impoverished person, yet welfare regards its clients as passive reactors to stimuli, especially the coldest stimulus of all—cash.

A WORLD WITHOUT WELFARE

PROCEEDINGS OF A
FAMILY RESEARCH COUNCIL SYMPOSIUM,
WASHINGTON, D.C., DECEMBER 13, 1995

WITH A PREFACE BY
GARY L. BAUER

FAMILY RESEARCH COUNCIL

DAVID M. WAGNER, EDITOR

PUBLISHED BY FAMILY RESEARCH COUNCIL
WASHINGTON, D.C.
1997

PARTICIPANTS

Don E. Eberly   Urban Miyares

Peter Ferrara   Rev. Donald Moore

David Frum   Kris Mauren

Michael Gerson   Michael Novak

Dr. Virgil Gulker   Marvin Olasky

Heather R. Higgins   John M. Perkins

Rev. Donald Marino   Robert Rector

Jennifer E. Marshall   Terrence Scanlon

William R. Mattox, Jr.   Rev. Robert Sirico, CSP

Adam Meyerson   John P. Walters

Don Michele   Robert L. Woodson, Sr.

Family Research Council is an independent, non-profit, education and research organization dedicated to ensuring that the interests of the family are considered and respected in the formation of public policy. Through a wide variety of publications and other communications tools, the Council works to create in the legislative, executive, and judicial branches of the federal government an understanding of the family's role in preserving civilization. Family Research Council also works to educate and inform citizens of how they can promote Biblical principles in our culture.

Alleviation of poverty requires the formation and maintenance of stable families, yet welfare makes fathers superfluous and encourages impoverished mothers to "marry" the government.

Alleviation of poverty requires that our society's most powerful motive for caring—the teaching and example of Jesus Christ, the Savior who was born poor, lived poor, and befriended the poor—be unleashed, yet welfare is burdened with the Supreme Court's decades-long quest to excise religious belief, enforced by ever-vigilant organizations that would rather see poverty perpetuated than see it relieved by people of faith.

Between these covers you will find conference papers, the transcript of an awards ceremony honoring people who are making a real difference for the poor in their communities, and personal testimonies by the award recipients. By reading them, you will learn in depth how the concept of "civil society" is being revived by young conservative theorists, and how certain particular individuals and organizations are making that concept come alive.

The speakers are of many different types, but from that variety certain points come consistently: 1) Government-directed welfare is not second-best to private charity—it is a malignant competitor to it, 2) the need for localism: the federal government, state governments, and even local governments are too far removed from the communities where the poor will find help if they find it at all, and 3) the need for faith.

The speakers from this conference, and hundreds of thousands like them, are the future. Someday, historians will write of FDR's and LBJ's welfare state the way they write of Diocletian's. Our modern-day Diocletians will pass away as the old ones did—vanishing in the wake of new leaders who proclaim, "In this sign ye shall conquer."

Gary L. Bauer, *President*
Family Research Council

ACKNOWLEDGMENTS

In planning Family Research Council's World Without Welfare symposium, I was unusually blessed by the efforts and dedication of many others who gave from the heart and without whom the symposium would not have been possible.

I owe thanks first to my dear friends and colleagues at Family Research Council. Paul Fitzpatrick helped coordinate foundation support and has provided much personal encouragement to me at all the critical crossroads. Anne Fitzpatrick helped with logistical coordination and made an appearance the day of the event. Anne Redd cheerfully kept the trains running, and Scott Potter was both a consummate professional and a kind friend as he managed the mailing lists.

Many thanks to Sharon Johnson for help with hotel coordination, Rosanne Dupras for help with registration, and Amy Dixon and Loralei Gilliam for photography at the Willard. I remember with much gratitude all the other FRC staff—Kristi Hamrick, Doug Werk, Bob Morrison, Jennifer A. Marshall, Cathy Deeds, and several others—who took time out of their busy work days to be there.

Virgil Gulker, Executive Director of Kids Hope USA, and Carl Herrick, Executive Director of the Daylight Foundation, provided photographs for a display that reminded us of all the children and the volunteers to whom our effort was dedicated. Dan Donehey of Donehey and Associates did an outstanding job with the audiotapes and transcripts, and Ramesh Ponnuru deserves a word of thanks for making mention of the symposium in *National Review*.

I reserve my warmest personal thanks for all the speakers who graciously responded to my invitation because they knew the importance of the topic. I thank Kris Mauren of the Acton Institute for choosing the symposium to be the site for the presentation of Acton's 1995 Samaritan Awards. The award winners reminded us why we had gathered and humbled us with their stories.

Special thanks go also to Charles A. Donovan for overseeing the production of this book, Clint Chadbourne for graphic design, and Gina Dalfonzo for proofreading, all of Family Research Council.

I especially must thank Bill Mattox, Vice President for Policy at Family Research Council at the time of the symposium. He was the first to validate the vision, and he provided critical encouragement every step of the way. A heart full of thanks, Bill, for your wise leadership and your good example.

Abundant thanks, too, to my dear friend Deanna Carlson— FRC's Welfare Policy Associate at the time and now Community Outreach Coordinator. She came in answer to His call, and she stayed to implement the project we described in barest detail at the symposium.

To the God who calls every one of us, I give all my thanks for the work He began at Family Research Council and continues to do.

In the time that has passed since the symposium, I have received a phone call every few months from a woman who watched and listened in the audience as these speeches were delivered. We met for the first time the day of the symposium. When she calls, we chat for awhile about things of mutual interest. Then she says, "I just called to make sure you remember that God gave us a vision that day."

Yes, Portia, I remember, and He is still at work.

Jennifer E. Marshall
September 1997

Jennifer E. Marshall organized the World Without Welfare symposium while serving as Welfare Policy Analyst at Family Research Council. Shortly after the symposium, she became a Bradley Fellow at the Heritage Foundation. She is now Executive Director of the Alliance for Belief in Action.

INTRODUCTION

On December 13, 1995, Family Research Council gathered a diverse group of people united by one common concern: the overwhelming damage done to the hearts and souls of our nation's needy by the welfare bureaucracy that is supposed to be helping them.

Protestants and Catholics, libertarians and social conservatives, Washington policy makers and grass-roots practitioners, all agreed that the welfare state has broken families and broken hearts, has destroyed incentives for today and hopes for tomorrow, and has created a caste of those who, from generation to generation, don't know anyone who's married, don't know anyone who works, and don't know anyone who cares.

All agreed that the deepest needs of those trapped by welfare are not met by a government check, food stamps, and utility vouchers, but rather by love, nurture, and a sense of significance— just as they are for all mankind. All agreed that government is not merely ill-equipped to meet those needs but even is destructive of the efforts of individuals and entities well-suited to serve. All agreed that repairing the damage can only be done one-on-one, at the local level, by the family, by the church, and by the community.

Family Research Council's Symposium, "A World Without Welfare," stirred a new dialogue at the community level by focusing on the role that government continues to play in promoting cultural decay. The Symposium discredited failed and morally bankrupt policies, provided a coherent philosophical framework for social conservatives' involvement in dismantling the welfare state, and created a sense of urgency about the need to cultivate charitable alternatives.

Having acknowledged that a groundswell of non-political activity can create political pressure for reform, we also emphasized that the existence of a government safety net inevitably dampens enthusiasm for charitable efforts.

Thus, we encouraged social conservatives to work on two tracks at once: volunteering time at local charities and joining economic conservatives in lobbying for cuts in government programs. Whether or not we agree that curbing government is sufficient to restore the good society, conservatives of all stripes can agree that an activist state creates conditions that will not be conducive to the rebirth of moral rigor.

We concluded that limiting government is itself a moral imperative, made necessary by the fact that public policy can undermine—but never instill—virtue. Rather than seeking to use government to promote traditionalist ends, we must relimit government to expand the freedom that fosters individual decisions to serve one another.

The fusion of the ideas of libertarians and social conservatives and of policy makers and activists is creating a cultural force of great power. Family Research Council has been proud to play a part in generating that restorative force.

Jennifer E. Marshall with Leslie Carbone

KEYNOTE ADDRESS ON LIBERTY AND VIRTUE

Introduction

Jennifer E. Marshall, *welfare policy analyst,*
Family Research Council

We have quite a lot of work before us before we can say the phrase *world without welfare* and mean more than the title of a one-day symposium. This day will be devoted not only to arguing that the welfare state needs new limits, but also to outlining what will be required of us as social conservatives in particular, if we are to realize those limits.

Even so, I would also like us to keep in mind that we're really not asking for radical new innovations. We are asking for a return to the vision of our Founders. The fact that a call for relimiting government and rebuilding society should sound so radical to our modern ears is really a testimony to how far we have strayed, especially in the last 30 years under Great Society programs. One of the Founders' most important insights is that the freedom of individuals and the vitality of communities are not competitive, but intertwined. That assumption has staked out a large plot of common ground that is to be shared by all conservatives of all stripes.

If there is an overarching theme for this morning's sessions, it is building bridges between libertarians and social conservatives. Not because that is an interesting theoretical exercise, even though it is, but because we have a job to do that will require a collaborative effort. This is not a job, though, that can be done inside the Beltway. The most important work really has to be done by people like Johnny Goodnight in Los Angeles, Carl Herrick in Baton Rouge, and Wayne Gordon in Illinois and all the other people like them who are also here today.

In the course of the afternoon, we are going to turn from the Beltway to the heartland, and from abstract philosophy to the very practical issues that are involved in recruiting rank and file

America to build up the mass of civil institutions that will have to be in place before Jeffersonian democracy is once again the American way of life.

Our first speaker is Dr. Michael Novak, who currently holds the George Frederick Jewett Chair in Religion and Public Policy at the American Enterprise Institute, where he also serves as Director of Social and Political Studies. He has written 25 influential books in the philosophy and theology of culture, including *Belief and Unbelief, The Rise of the Unmeltable Ethnics,* and *The Catholic Ethic and the Spirit of Capitalism.* He's also the author of numerous monographs and over 500 articles and reviews.

Dr. Novak's writings have appeared in every major Western language, and his book *The Spirit of Democratic Capitalism* has been reprinted often, especially in Latin America, and was published underground in Poland in 1984. On May 4, 1994, Dr. Novak received the 24th Templeton Prize for Progress in Religion at Buckingham Palace. He's an ideal keynote speaker for this symposium, not just because he's written a marvelous defense of civil society in *The Catholic Ethic and the Spirit of Capitalism,* and not just because he understands the need to bridge the gap between intellectuals and people, which is the title of an essay he wrote in the 1960s, but because he himself embodies an ideal combination of intellectual rigor and a keen sense of humanity. It's very much a privilege to welcome him this morning.

THE CASE
FOR REBUILDING
CIVIL SOCIETY

Dr. Michael Novak, *George Frederick Jewett Chair in Religion and Public Policy, American Enterprise Institute*
Thank you for allowing me to come to this important conference and to share in the really central work of the Family Research Council.

When we talk about welfare, it's good to make a distinction right up front. The war on poverty in the mid-1960s did make a real difference for the elderly, for the sick, and for the disabled that we shouldn't disregard.

It was in certain aspects a great success for the elderly, for example. In 1965, the largest group of the poor were those over age 65. In the rhetoric of John Kennedy's campaign in the early '60s, when Michael Harrington's book [*The Other America*] was being bruited about, pictures of the poor on the covers of *Life* Magazine or *Look* or other magazines of the time were inevitably pictures of the elderly. If you look today, by almost every measure, the elderly are almost entirely out of poverty. If there are elderly poor, it is because they are not hooked up to systems that are there to help them.

Moreover, in 1965 we counted as elderly all people who were 65 or over. Today, the real worrisome part of elderly is the *elderly* elderly, the over 85s, whose numbers have increased to proportions that are comparable to the proportions of those over 65 just 30 years ago.

Now the financial aspects of this accomplishment, the funding mechanisms that we used, are still serious problems, and thus we are quite worried about the future of Medicare and even the future of Social Security. The programs in and of themselves were a great success, and I think it's worth setting that aside from our discussion for the moment, though the funding mechanisms and so on need a great deal of attention. Similarly, the position of the disabled and the sick is much better than it was just 30 years ago.

There is, nonetheless, a sense in which welfare programs have dramatically failed. When we say welfare, we typically mean the part of the poverty programs that were addressed to young people, young adults between the ages of 16 and 45 especially. The chief program that has been worrisome has been Aid for Families with Dependent Children (AFDC). In the late 1930s when it was founded, AFDC was predominantly a program for widows. For many years afterward, 95 percent or more of the people who received aid under that program were widows whose husbands were killed in mining accidents or mill accidents or whatever. Then, after 1965, with great rapidity, AFDC became a program predominantly for young single women having children out of wedlock. When we say *welfare* in America, when the public hears that word, that's the part of the problem they almost always fix on, and it is very well worth fixing on.

The Family Research Council is one of the organizations that grew up to respond to the insight that the vast majority of the poor are in families—often, I should add, unformed families, families not based on marriage—and that if you want to help the poor, the surest and most direct route is by helping the family. If the family is healthy and functioning well, you don't need what used to be called the Department of Health, Education and Welfare. That's what the family does when it's functioning well. When the family isn't functioning well, nothing that all the departments of health, education and welfare do can make up for the loss. The family is the only department of health, education and welfare that works, and when it works, you don't need the other one.

One of the insights that the public senses but that many critics of welfare reform don't seem to grasp is the sheer devastation wrought by the programs we launched in 1965. Those of us who supported the war on poverty, as I certainly did, did not warn the citizenry, "If you adopt this program we will bring you a 600 percent increase in violent crime and a 500 percent increase in births out of wedlock." That wasn't our intention. Nobody foresaw that happening or wanted it to happen, but that's what did happen. In other words, it's important to grasp the damage that welfare is doing.

The reason for being concerned about welfare reform today—and trying to imagine a world without welfare—is not budgetary. It's not its cost. Its cost is not insuperable. If it were doing good, we would gladly support it. Most of us would. I think the vast majority would. What's disconcerting to people is that it's manifestly doing harm. To put it another way, it's not achieving the good it set out to achieve, and the problems it set out to address are not getting better.

Witness John Kennedy's statement in early 1963 about the first move toward welfare reform, which later became the War on Poverty after his death. He said it was intended to strengthen the American family, to put an end to juvenile delinquency. Can you imagine how quaint a term that later would become? Who speaks of juvenile delinquency? That's a term from the '50s and '60s. That's long gone. It's violent crime. Juvenile delinquency was ended: it became violent crime. Such were the intentions of the program, and it failed to achieve them.

I want to warn you to be careful here, too. It's very hard to show that welfare has caused all the civic destruction that has happened since 1965 among families we intended to help. So many other things happened, television and affluence and urban renewal. It's hard to find any one explanation. At a minimum, one can say that welfare in this narrower sense that I'm using was aimed to address these problems and that it didn't succeed. The problems have gotten worse.

At the very least, welfare didn't provide the help to the younger poor that it was supposed to provide, though you can see that the situation of the elderly is manifestly better than it was in 1965. When my parents were very ill in the last days before their deaths, they were helped by Medicare to benefit from medical research that didn't even exist 30 years ago and much more expensive procedures, which were covered. The family was by and large spared that very heavy expense over the last weeks of their lives. It was wonderful to able to be present with them in those last weeks. They themselves many times thanked God that they lived so well and so long in ways they never imagined that they would, having seen what happened to their parents. That part of the program was a success, but the part of the program aimed at younger people left us in a situation in many ways worse than it was 30 years ago.

In Washington, D.C., where we're meeting, 64 percent of all pregnancies end in abortion. Of those young children who survive, 70 percent plus are born out of wedlock. Now, it's not simply that they're born out of wedlock as if that's merely a personal harm to them. It also means in reality that these youngsters will be born without the presence of half of an extended family. That is, they will, generally speaking, lack grandparents, uncles, aunts on one side of the family. On the woman's side of the family, perhaps the family will be supportive. Usually it is, but it may not be. Already the child's world is cut in half from what a child would normally have.

If the child is born into a household disconnected from the world of work and disconnected from neighbors who work, that child is born without connections to the world of work. The prognosis for later employment is very poor. The health prognosis is poor. The prognosis for finishing school is poor. The prognosis for involvement in the criminal justice system is very high. In this city, the chances of involvement in the criminal justice system by age 30 are about 80 percent.

Those who want to continue welfare as we know it carry on their shoulders a very heavy burden. I believe in this respect that even the Catholic bishops who are resisting some of the move for reform are not facing as directly as they ought to the moral responsibility that accrues to them for continuing the program as it now is.

One of the worst features of the welfare program as it now is, especially for the young, is that it takes good, healthy young people, able to be creative and energetic and to show initiative, and leaves them in a state of dependency in two respects. First, many of them are not there to be able to take care of their children or their parents. In other words, the healthy young adults are usually the ones on whom the elderly depend, not on whom children depend. Since for the most part they are not working, they do not have the means to take care of those who depend on them. Second, this seems to bring with it certain psychic wounds because many such people are not able to be independent themselves. They throw themselves on the care of the government, on the care of the larger society, both for the care of their dependents and for their own care. Then there's a third sense of dependency for a very high percentage of them. While their schooling is free, they don't complete schooling. Many become involved in alcohol or drugs and in other sorts of behavior that is self-destructive.

In all three of these senses, we have learned since 1965 that poverty—that is, a lack of material resources—is not the worst consequence, but dependency in these three senses is much worse. It takes someone who ought to be a self-governing citizen, self-reliant, brave, showing initiative, creating jobs, and leaves her in the state of counting on others for the most basic things. I hate to mention this term, but generally it leaves them also with a great loss of self-esteem. In these cases, self-esteem is a very important reality to cope with. It's hard when you're not achieving to have a sense of a proper adult achievement.

America was never founded to be a society for dependent people. The American experiment is an experiment in self-government, and I want to talk about that in the second part of my remarks now.

What it means to have republican government is to have a government that allows most decisions, most social activities, to be undertaken by the citizens themselves. They're self-governing. They are able to manage their social lives. They are able to manage their social necessities. One of the most extraordinary things about the founding of this republic, commented on by Tocqueville 50 years after the founding, is the capacity of Americans to organize themselves to take care of their own needs.

My wife and I recovered the diary of an ancestor of hers. Believe it or not, his name was Charlie Brown. He was the son of the first Baptist missionary in the Iowa Territory before it became a state. Charles Brown writes in his diary day after day about the importance of individualism, the importance of the individual, but that's not what he describes. What's in his head is how much individual initiative it took to depart from the family back east near Syracuse and before that in Massachusetts and move out to this new territory where the plow had never yet cut the soil. When he arrived, it was buffalo grass. Not many people lived out there because the Native Americans who lived there used it mostly as a hunting ground. It was not for farming. Most passed through.

In any case, in talking about the individual, what day after day Brown describes is working on the farm of so-and-so putting up a barn. On another day, they're putting a bridge over a creek. On another day, they're putting up the equivalent of a city hall. On another day, they're working on the school. The substance of his days is working together with neighbors on projects to make their common life go, to make it work.

What I'm trying to establish is that this is the building of civil society. This is the building of the ability of human beings to live together in a good community when there's no government or only a very limited form of government. As Tocqueville says, this is the great advantage the Americans had. They were so lightly governed. The King and Parliament hardly paid them attention except to tax them. They were organized first into villages and townships; only much later into counties and states, and only after almost 200 years into a federal government. Americans learned how to conduct a social life for themselves before they had government.

Tocqueville also remarks that, at the time of the French revolution, there were not ten men in all France who were capable of practicing the art of association as Americans were. What he meant by that was that, in France, when something is needed, people turn to the state to do it. In Britain, people turn to the aristocracy to fund it. In America, they turned to one another. They formed associations.

Tocqueville formed the principle that the first law of democracy is the principle of association. The very first law is that it will only work where people are capable of self-government through forming their own associations and making communal decisions, social decisions, and figuring out the mechanisms to make them fairly and well.

In America people almost universally became practiced in the art of association. People formed associations, Tocqueville said, to send missionaries to the Antipodes, to build colleges, to put up buildings, to bring music to a village or town, to put on a musical. They form associations for every imaginable purpose. They didn't turn to government because in the early days there was no government to turn to, or else a government of very limited resources and very limited authority.

This is what our framers intended by the experiment in self-government of the people, by the people, for the people. You have to have a government, as the generation of our framers discovered when they were badly governed by the Articles of Confederation. They needed to form a more perfect union. Government is necessary. Their project was not an anti-government program. It was a matter of getting government right, and part of getting government right was to leave space for people to govern themselves, so that government as such would play as small a role as necessary.

That is the original and has been the continuing American experiment, and I think that the restlessness that we are seeing in the country is an urge to get back to something like that—to devolve, as the word has come to be used. Some of the powers that have accrued to the federal government did so only because of the great wars of the 20th century—the two world wars, which led to far more centralized government power and taxing power than anyone had earlier envisaged.

Now, on the law of association, it isn't quite right to say that all our social units are voluntary. Most are, but there are some that are natural, given to us by nature. One of those is the family.

I've already mentioned the centrality of the family, but let me give you one more little factoid that's impressive. In the United States, there are three things such that, if you do them, you have less than a 5 percent chance of being poor. One of them is to complete high school. It's free, but a substantial number of people don't do it. The second is to work full-time, even at a minimum wage job. The third is to get married and stay married. Just a very few years ago, only about 6 percent of married couple families were poor. Today, it's about 8 percent. Marriage alone gives you a 92 percent chance of getting out of poverty. The two incomes, in any case the support of two people, seem to have some financial and also psychological power that is of great assistance. Of course, with work and with at least the minimum of a high school education, you do very well. We see this being realized every day.

One of the things that has changed the argument in the country dramatically in the last 20 years is the influx of immigrants from very poor backgrounds from all over the world. They arrive poor financially, but in a short time are not poor. Their success through family and through work and their success in pushing their children in education has led them to move out of poverty, and restored our faith in the possibilities in the American system for helping the poor regularly to move out of poverty.

What sticks in the craw of Americans, in fact, is the vision before their eyes of so many people not moving out of poverty. That's what's uncharacteristic; that's what's unprecedented. That's what gives people the sense that the system is failing. The system is meant to move people out of poverty within a decade or so, a generation at most. When it's not doing that, that's what makes people say there is something wrong with the system, something we've done wrong in our design of it.

One thing that the experience of the last 20 years has taught us is that the welfare population does not have a racial profile. It's always wise to remind oneself that the vast majority of people who are poor and who are on welfare are white. The press often tries to portray this as a black problem, and they frequently show black people when they talk about welfare. But any of you who come from states with more rural settings, or states with smaller towns and cities, know about the increase in welfare among whites all over the United States. Even the increase of illegitimacy today among whites is now higher than it was when, in 1965, Senator Moynihan, who was at that time Assistant Secretary of Labor, declared it a disaster among blacks. It's now higher among whites and growing more rapidly than among blacks.

The family thus is one of the crucial places to apply our attention. This is not habitual among social scientists and American intellectuals in general. Political thought for the last 200 years has been more or less mesmerized by the two great discoveries of the last 200 years: the nation-state and the individual. For the first time in history, a great many individuals moved away from their families through migration or through the opening up of new occupations. They moved into occupations that were not traditional in their families. Sometimes they changed their religions from those of their families. Often they changed their places, moved away from their families. It's been a hugely migratory two centuries. All of us here are a part of that migration: the greatest migration in human history is the migration to the United States over a very short period. People became aware of separating from their families; they became acutely aware of being individuals.

Simultaneously, we had the formation of the nation-state. I'm oversimplifying, of course, but, by and large, progressives—liberals as we tend to call them in this country, but not in others—have, when presented with a problem, typically tended to think of a state solution for it. On the other side, conservatives faced with a problem typically have tried to think of something that the individual could do. Our social thought has been oscillating between these two extreme views, individualism and statism, overlooking the great dramatic middle in which most human life is lived.

I don't know about you, but practically the only place I get to be alone is on an airplane. I only get to be alone after I answer two questions. The person next to me always eventually says, "What do you do?"

I figured out the answer that stops most of them cold. I say, "I teach." Most of them have dreadful memories of school, and that usually ends the conversation right there.

A few of them are brave souls and they will say, showing their sophistication, "What do you teach?" I have a perfect answer for that, too.

I say, in as brief a voice as I can, "Humanities."

They say, "Oh."

That's it; I'm free. There are no committee meetings; there are no telephones, and for an hour and a half or four hours, or whatever it is, I have the first solitude I've had in days. The rest of the time seems to be spent in committees, and going to meetings. Most of the time is spent with other people.

American life is probably the most social life in the world. Increasingly one of the most difficult tasks in America is getting the whole family to sit down together at the dinner table, because somebody always has band practice or hockey practice, or somebody is always attending a meeting. If you want to get one night together, you almost have to enforce it, the way the Mormons do. It has to be a family night, when there are no other meetings, and everybody's home for this.

I had an Italian friend whom I once asked why he came to work in "Cleve-a-land," which is how he said it, and he said, *"Per fare fortuna"*—to make my fortune.

I said, "Why did you go back to Italy?"

He said, *"Per vivere"*—to live. In Italy, you take a shave and a haircut, two hours. America, eight minutes. In Italy, you have dinner all evening, four hours—that's normal. In America, in the evenings you're at meetings. He said the trouble with America is you work eight hours a day and then you go to eight hours of meetings.

We're a very social people, with our families and all the different organizations and groups that we belong to; we live a richly social life.

It's not a community life in the way the Europeans imagined community. When the Europeans imagine community, they always think of a village somewhere in the mountains where you didn't know anybody outside the village, where everybody shares the same faith and the same outlook, and families have known one another for hundreds of years and they were almost like family together. That's the European sense of community. It is not, I think, the highest sense of community. It's a lovely form of community, but it can be quite oppressive, and it is often xenophobic. It distresses others, and it is often repressive of the talents and abilities of rare people within it.

To pick up the theme I began with—the family, the association, the capacity of Americans to look around, see a need, and form an organization to meet it—that is what a world without welfare is going to call on Americans to do more and more.

My friend Phil Merrill, who is the publisher of *Washingtonian* and other publications in this city and a shrewd observer of life, predicts that in the next 20 years there's going to be the most massive transfer of wealth in the history of this republic. He points out, "Just look at pictures of the city of Washington 30 years ago and overlay them with a photograph of today. Look at how many new buildings have gone up. Look at areas like Bethesda and Falls Church and the whole surrounding area that were residential communities and today are bustling communities with factories and offices of every sort all over. Think of the fortunes that have been made in auto dealerships and by owners of buildings." Most of that money, Phil maintains, is going to go to charity. Most of it's going to go into the greatest outbreak of philanthropy that the country has ever known, and that the world has ever known.

The stock market, in this year, in 12 months, has gone up one trillion dollars of new wealth. It's just astonishing what is going on around us. New industries, new technologies that were not even thought of are coming on-line. When people talk about our children being worse off than we were, when we grew up, that our children are not going to have the same opportunities, they are overlooking the wealth that, for our children, starts in the homes, in home ownership. Then there are pensions, and other hidden forms of wealth that are not usually counted. When you see these comparisons of wealth and so forth, they almost all leave out homes, your personal possessions, your compact disc player. What most of us count as our wealth isn't counted. What they count as wealth is stock ownership, which some 20 to 30 million American families have, but not everybody. Those studies reach a necessary conclusion that wealth is concentrated because they only count a certain kind of wealth. Most of the other kinds of wealth they do not count.

Now, the last requirement of a self-governing society— beyond the capacity to form families and to form associations to meet whatever needs we discern—is the personal requirement. The project of self-government will only succeed with a certain kind of people. It's chimerical—a fantasy, Madison said—to imagine that a republic can be made to work without virtue. Now, by *virtue,* the framers meant certain habits, and, in fact, certain particular habits, that a people has to have if it wishes to be a free people. They thought there are peoples on this planet who are not capable of liberty. They do not have the habits of self-government. They will not be able to make self-government work. Now what did they mean by *self-government?* They meant the capacity for two actions in particular. Out of all the things human beings do, there are two that are most particular to us as human beings. One is the capacity for reflection or deliberation. The other is the capacity for choosing. The two together are what make liberty.

The capacity for deliberation or for reflection is a simple one. I can best explain it in relationship to the two cats we have at home. I hate cats, but our daughters, when they were six and seven, each brought home a cat and begged us to adopt them, lest they meet a terrible fate. They promised they would take care of the cats forever; the parents would never have to do anything. The only problem is that our children are grown up and gone, and we still have the cats. We can't even leave home without finding a cat sitter. One is orange; one is black and white: *Pépé Le Purr* and *Le Beau de L'Orange,* as the children named them. One is thin, and one is fat; one is quick, and one is slow and dimwitted. There's no question that our cats have different personalities.

On the other hand, there's one thing we never have to worry about, as we do have to worry with our kids—What career are they going to choose?

Our children act. They think of things that we wish they wouldn't think of. Humans do; cats behave. They behave as cats always have, I think, since the time the first one posed for the Sphinx. In 5,000 years, cats have done nothing original. It's behavior. Our children are capable of reflecting on the future, seeing alternatives, and choosing among them. They're capable of looking back on the past and finding things that they're sorry for and things that they're pleased with and happy about. That capacity to reflect is crucial to liberty.

Our framers distinguished between two different kinds of liberty, as Tocqueville points out in the first pages of *Democracy in America:* the liberty proper to animals and the liberty proper to human beings. Our cats just do what they please. Whatever instinct tells them to do, they do. They cannot do other than obey their instincts. Human beings have several different sets of instincts at war with one another. Human beings have to choose which instincts to follow. The capacity for self-government is the capacity to choose under the light of reflection and deliberation.

Let me close on this note. The French built the Statue of Liberty to reflect this new idea of liberty. The idea of *liberté* failed in the French Revolution, but the idea of liberty succeeded in North America, the kind of liberty that Pope John Paul II, ever since his first visit to America, has insisted on calling "ordered liberty." That, he said, is the great contribution of American civilization to world civilization: the concept of the practice and institutions of ordered liberty.

The French didn't know what sort of monument to build. They wanted to build one of the great monuments of the world. They formed a committee. Since they were French, the first decision was easy. It would be the figure of a woman. Even apart from their inclinations, a woman is the symbol of liberty in French iconography from at least the fifth century. Not the young male with a weapon, but a woman, wisdom, Lady Wisdom. She may carry the banner, the *tricouleur.* In her right arm, they put the torch of reason against the mist and fog of bigotry and passion and ignorance. In her other arm, they put the book of the law.

Liberty under reason, liberty under law. It's a distinctive understanding of liberty. To be free is to act from reflection and deliberation, which is hard. Often we act out of instinct, out of passion, out of impulse. To act, as Jefferson has been often described as having done and Washington is always described as having done, soberly with reflection, with self-mastery, is the very model of self-government. Now how, Madison asked, can you have self-government in the republic if you don't have self-government in the citizens? You can't imagine that a people incapable of self-government in their private lives can practice self-government in their public lives.

What we need to understand is that that is our model for the poor. It always has been—just as it has been for the rich, for everybody. The capacity for self-government, the capacity for a certain independence, for reflective and deliberate behavior, and the acceptance of consequences of decisions. That's exactly what our current welfare programs have destroyed in large numbers of people. What poor people coming from around the world, seeing this, tell themselves is: "Stay off welfare: It's a honey trap. It can so easily destroy."

Well, when we talk about reconstituting civil society, that's our agenda. It's an agenda with a very full spectrum. Everything from recovering the habits that Bill Bennett tried to bring to our attention in *The Book of Virtues,* to renewing the spirit of volunteerism, the habit of Americans to look around and see what needs doing, and then do it themselves without turning to government, and to form organizations on a massive scale if necessary, as the Red Cross has become, or whatever scale is necessary to handle the problem. If we have to have government help, then the agenda is to find ways of having the government help indirectly rather than directly, rather than giving direct subsidies, to find an indirect way of helping institutions that encourage the independent, self-reliant, community-minded behavior that is proper to self-government.

We need a whole new imagination about what we're going to ask of government and how we're going to ask it to help. We know that, in a society as mobile and intercontinental as we are, there are going to be people who fall through the net. Families aren't going to be there to help them because they're at a distance. In this sense, we understand there has to be a welfare net of some kind. But how to provide this help? It does not have to be done in the manner in which it has been done for the last 30 years. We've succeeded for the elderly, but it was a grand failure, despite all good intentions, for young people. Our agenda is a very large one, and it's useful as we begin these reflections for the day to keep in mind how many different things we have to do at once. It's an entire rethinking, reformulating or reconstituting, of the American experiment, something that Jefferson said that we ought to do every 18 and one-third years just on principle.

DEBATE: BUILDING A COALITION TO RELIMIT GOVERNMENT AND REBUILD CIVIL SOCIETY

Jennifer E. Marshall, *moderator*

David Frum's writing has appeared in *The Wall Street Journal, The New York Times, The Washington Post, The Atlantic Monthly, Commentary, Harper's,* the *Times Literary Supplement, The New Republic,* and *The London Spectator.* He's a contributing editor at *The Weekly Standard* and a Senior Fellow at the Manhattan Institute. The most important fact about David Frum is that he's the author of *Dead Right,* a book described by William F. Buckley as "the most refreshing ideological experience in a generation" and one that I think has almost certainly framed the conservative debate for the next generation. It began with a deceptively simple thesis: that the size of government matters and that it may in fact matter most if you are a cultural conservative.

While Mr. Frum focuses on the extent to which the welfare state has eclipsed the "tough old American character, the self-reliant, self-controlled, hard working and patriotic American of old," as he put it in the preface, Father Sirico's work often focuses on a kinder, softer side of libertarianism. When libertarians talk of individual freedom, they often make it sound like atomism, without explaining that freedom also liberates the human spirit to express its social nature, the social nature that Dr. Novak described this morning. Lord Acton wished to teach man to defend liberty more for the love of virtue and charity than as a claim of right or an end in itself, and that's very much a goal that Father Sirico shares. He's the President of the Acton Institute for the Study of Religion and Liberty. His writings on religious, political, economic, and social issues have been published in a variety of journals including the *Wall Street Journal, Forbes,* the *London Financial Times,* and many others. In 1990, Father Sirico was inducted into a society founded by Hayek in 1947 to strengthen the principles and the practice of a free society. Welcome Father Sirico and David Frum for a conversation about relimiting government.

David Frum, author, Dead Right

Shortly before the 1994 elections, a pollster for the League of Women Voters in Chicago told me about a troubling fact she'd noticed. When her group called Chicago area voters on the telephone and asked them to name the top two or three election issues in that cycle, they heard familiar answers: taxes, crime, education, jobs. When they gathered smaller groups of Chicagoans together for longer discussions, the talk always shifted away from the headline issues of the day and toward deeper, more nameless anxieties, that society had somehow lost its way, that America no longer made sense, that the future had turned dark and menacing.

The pollster was made uncomfortable by this sort of talk. This wasn't politics, at any rate not the sort of politics the League of Women Voters understood. It is, however, the sort of politics that the people in this room understand. It is the sort of anxiety that fuels today's discussion. When we talk about social reforms, when we talk about welfare reforms, behind it all is a concern not just that individual programs are malfunctioning, that the cost of Medicaid is growing too fast, or that AFDC confronts some people with perverse incentives. What people fear is that the whole structure of American society, from the wealthiest to the poorest, has somehow gone awry, and we sense that the deepest institutions of American government, institutions that were created in their original form by very wise men, but that have been altered by less wise men, are in some way connected, are at fault in this disturbing evolution of the American system.

That is particularly worrying now, because this ought to be such a happy time. For the first time since the Japanese invaded Manchuria in 1931, Americans live in a world free of any threat to their security. The economy is strong; the job market may be more volatile than it used to be, but it still delivers real prosperity to those willing to work hard. Some six million American families now enjoy incomes of more than $100,000 a year, more than six times as many as in 1967. Middle class families, despite the talk of income stagnation, enjoy an unprecedented abundance of goods and services. Over the past 20 years, life expectancy has lengthened by three and a half years, a remarkable growth in such a short period of time. The number of Americans who have traveled overseas has doubled. As recently as 1980, only 20 percent of American grocery stores stocked fresh fruits and vegetables year round. Today, more than 80 percent do; that's a luxury that, in times past, not even kings and emperors could have dreamed up. The only Americans to lack indoor plumbing nowadays are *New Yorker* staff writers on sabbatical in the Adirondacks.

After inflation, a long distance telephone call costs about one-tenth of what it did in 1974. I'm just old enough to remember when a journalist could persuade a secretary to interrupt her boss's meeting by whispering dramatically over the phone, "It's long distance." I don't recommend you try that trick now.

Some observe this cornucopia of prosperity and suggest that Americans quit flagellating themselves, quit minutely inspecting the character of their poor, quit worrying that something has gone terribly wrong with the American experiment, and simply be grateful for all they possess. That's certainly a pardonable reaction that contains some seeds of wisdom. But if we believe in democracy, we should take seriously the old principle that the foot knows best where the shoe pinches. When Americans tell us that they are concerned about the functioning of their welfare system, if Americans feel anxiety and dread and spiritual emptiness in the midst of all their wealth, perhaps we should hearken to them.

Even if we don't, one could nonetheless itemize a list of horrors every bit as long as the list of achievements I've ticked off. Dependency, illegitimacy, crime, child abuse, suicide, abortion, all these leading cultural indicators, as Bill Bennett has cleverly termed them, are flashing warnings at us. They flash most alarmingly from the poorer sections of American prosperity.

Even in the middle class, families have gained their new prosperity largely by sending wives and mothers into the marketplace. More than half of all mothers whose youngest child is less than 12-months-old are now at work outside the home. Thirty percent of American children under age five spend their days in the care of a non-relative. What kind of people do we expect these abandoned children to grow into?

Most ominously of all, the reaction to the O.J. Simpson acquittal, the rallying to an anti-Semitic demagogue by half a million men on the mall of the Capitol, the radicalization of primary and secondary school curricula, the widening use of languages other than English on ballots and government documents, all these things call into question whether the United States remains any longer bound by a common nationhood. This is an issue of paramount importance to poor Americans, since it is in the name of common nationhood that the poorest Americans make their claim on the wealthiest Americans. After all, Americans do not tax themselves very generously to support the poor of Peru or Rwanda. They do tax themselves generously to support their own poor. The only reason they can be expected to do that is that they feel that these people belong, along with them, to one nation, and members of nations share responsibilities to each other.

The voters of Chicago, in other words, may perceive reality a little more clearly than the pollsters of the League of Women Voters do. Many conservatives have come to see the world the way the Chicagoans do. This can sometimes breed a dangerous passivity, because they look at the intense fights being waged in the Congress—fights over the budget, over Medicare, over agriculture subsidies, and yes, even the particular details of welfare reforms—and they feel a striking lack of enthusiasm for them. They feel almost a surge of boredom and wonder, asking themselves: For this I'm supposed to wake up early to drive voters to the polls next November, simply to shrink government by a few percentage points? I've come here today to tell you: yes, for this. Here's why.

There's a vital connection, and a powerful connection, between the size and scope of the federal government and the social pathologies that alarm those voters in Chicago and alarm us all. It would be ridiculously simple-minded to claim that big government alone causes social decay. Germany's government is much bigger and more intrusive than America's, but the streets of Düsseldorf do not echo to the rattle of drive-by shootings. The causes of America's social troubles are, as the social scientists say, exogenous. They originate in deep elements of the American character, the ideals of individualism. They originate also in the peculiar and historic tendency of Americans to resort to violence to solve their problems. They originate in the shift from an industrial to a post-industrial economy, to changing ideas about women and their roles, to the weakening grip of organized religion, to immigration patterns, to the long shadow of slavery and segregation, and a dozen other profound social forces. These forces express themselves as they do, their effects are channeled and directed as they are, by public policy.

Falling airfares and economic turmoil in Latin America may bring more Hispanic immigrants to Florida and Texas, but it was public policy that made welfare available to them immediately upon their arrival, that segregated their children in bilingual classes, that grouped them together as a legally privileged caste for affirmative action purposes, and that decided it was the obligation of the government to learn their language rather than their obligation to learn the common language of the United States.

The erosion of religious authority and the sexual revolution may deserve the ultimate blame for the explosion in divorce rates in the 1970s and 1980s. But would those rates have rocketed quite so high if the expansion of state and local government employment had not made available to millions of women well-paid white-collar jobs at precisely the same time that male-dominated blue-collar job categories were suffering unprecedented losses of pay, security, and prestige? If the tough new enforcement of child support obligations had not made it possible for a woman to expect to collect an oafish husband's income without enduring his unwelcome presence? If Medicaid, housing subsidies, welfare, and government-subsidized college loans did not reassure absconding fathers that their kids could survive without them?

The force driving the social trends that offend conservatives, and dependency most of all, is the welfare function of modern government. Attempting to solve those problems while government continues to exacerbate them is like coping with a sewer main explosion by bolting all the manhole covers to the pavement.

Now, I know that, right now, there are conservatives who would like to try to deal with America's social pathologies without limiting American government. Patrick Buchanan is right now engaging in a fascinating test of the electoral possibilities of a social conservatism separate from the traditional Republican commitment to smaller government. His television commercials, now being aired in New Hampshire and Arizona, attack the Republican congressional majority for its attempt to slow the growth of Medicare spending. "Why not cut foreign aid instead?" Mr. Buchanan asks, although he must know that the U.S. could eliminate every single one of its foreign aid programs, including the cost of the much-maligned Mexican loan guarantees, and the resulting reduction of the one and one-half trillion dollar federal budget would look like a rounding error. Mr. Buchanan explains himself by saying that he's attempting to reach the conservatives of the heart, working men and women who do not thrill to the austere elegance of economic formulae. It's not a foolish idea, not at least from an electoral view.

If conservatism is to be a philosophy of governing, it must do more than gain votes; it must offer actual solutions, practicable solutions to the social problems of the day, and that is what a social conservatism that has made its peace with big government cannot do. It defies my imagination to envision how the American personality that conservatives cherish—self-reliant, self-confident, uncomplaining, ingenious—can flourish in an environment that heaps rewards on dependency, misconduct, whining, and incompetence. You can't raise Victorian personalities in a Great Society state.

I do not mean, however, to criticize social conservatives alone. Alongside Mr. Buchanan, there is a candidate who has championed economic conservatism as exclusively as Mr. Buchanan has championed social conservatism: Senator Phil Gramm. Despite an excellent voting record on the issues that social conservatives care about, Senator Gramm, from the beginning of his campaign, has repeatedly refused to interest himself very deeply in their issues. In that refusal, he's encountered the great weakness of economic conservatism taken on its own. Unless it is linked to the concerns of social decay and social dislocation that animate all American citizens, it ignites strikingly little enthusiasm. Senator Gramm may perceive a big and expensive government as an imminent threat to the liberties of the American people. So do I. But the American people clearly think otherwise. Freedom in the abstract is too abstract for most of them.

It might have been possible for Senator Gramm to move the voting public by linking his great theme of big government to issues that worry Americans more, to income stagnation and to the decline of social order in American cities, but, so far, he has not managed to do so. Given the public's mistrust of Republican sincerity on the income stagnation issue, there's little reason to hope that Senator Gramm will ever manage to connect with them. Had he or some other economic conservative spoken with simplicity and passion to the link between hypertrophic government and social decay, who knows? A real conservative might well be on his way to the White House by now. Instead, conservatives across the country have divided their loyalties between the socially conservative Mr. Buchanan and the economically conservative Senator Gramm, to the immediate advantage of Senator Bob Dole, and to the ultimate profit, I fear, of President Clinton.

That's a pessimistic reading of the Republican political scene, but I am not a pessimist in general, and I don't think other conservatives should be pessimistic either. I see two immense demographic changes ahead, changes that should transform the whole country—from the richest to the poorest—for the better in many of the ways that the Baby Boom transformed it for the worse.

First, sometime around May 1996, the first of the children born to American soldiers returning from World War II will turn 50. Over the following 15 years, an enormous cohort of Americans will be entering the years in which their own mortality becomes impossible to deny, even for this, the most immature generation in history. The aging of the Baby Boomers will, I predict, introduce a new note of reserve into a licentious culture. An old joke has it that a conservative is a liberal with teenage daughters. If that's right, America will soon be teeming with enormous numbers of conservatives.

A second coming demographic transformation follows from the first. Think of the Baby Boom in the shape of a triangle. There were more babies born in 1947 than in 1946, more in 1948 than in 1947, and more in 1949 than in 1948, and so on. That boring fact takes on great significance when you remember that women typically marry or take up relationships with men a few years older than themselves. For 15 years now, we've heard women complain of a man shortage. Well, it was real. The women born between 1950 and 1955 faced a much smaller pool of eligible men, men born between 1945 and 1950. The women born between 1955 and 1960, face a smaller pool of men born between 1950 and 1955. Under these conditions, it was easy for men to demand what might be called a Sexual New Deal: more sex for less commitment.

Now look at what's ahead. There were fewer babies born in 1965 than in 1960, fewer in 1970 than in 1965, fewer in 1975 than in 1970. It is now men who will face a woman shortage, which means, I think, that the American sexual landscape will soon be transformed. The Sexual New Deal has run its course. Today's 20-year-old girls will find it much easier than their 40-year-old aunts to persuade their boyfriends to marry them, easier to insist on having children earlier rather than later, easier to marry men willing to let them exit the work force when their children are young, and this will be true, again, at all levels of society. I rather suspect, with the examples of their unhappy aunts before them, that today's young women will demand those things.

For this renaissance of traditional family values to occur, for this renaissance that is already imbedded in the demographic facts, American government must mend its ways. It must begin to remove the artificial obstacles it has put in the way of a successful life and repeal its malign incentives: not via just welfare reform, as crucial as that is, but also by equalizing tax rates for single-earner and two-career families, especially in the lower income echelons; equalizing the deductibility of institutional and home child care; removing subsidies to quasi-marital status; toughening the terms of welfare; and rethinking the rules of divorce. There is an immense family agenda being pursued by small-government conservatives. Quite frankly, I very much doubt that there is any other sort of conservative family agenda that will do any good at all.

Father Robert A. Sirico, CSP, *president,* The Acton Institute

It's good to note at the outset that in the minds of many people there is an oddity about the connection of a free-market philosophy and a moral and religious concern. In 1991, a survey was taken of clergy, and fewer than one in seven said that they believed that economics was important to their professional training. It seems that the old story that you can be so heavenly minded you're no earthly good sometimes applies in the religious profession.

I have attempted to probe the reason for this seeming dichotomy, and in addition to the fact that very few clergy ever study the discipline of economics, there are no formal courses required in any seminaries, that I am aware of, on economic topics, which, of course, doesn't stop religious leadership from pronouncing on economic matters.

In addition to that, I think there is a practical lacuna that exists between the mindset of people operating in a market economy who become personally familiar with the demands and the rigors of a market system and the mindset of religious leadership. That has to do with the practical way in which religious leaders come in touch with their money. We collect it. We pass baskets, and we redistribute money. If you do that long enough without reading about economics or having any extensive, practical involvement in a market economy, you begin to presume that what you collect and what you redistribute, the way in which you pay your bills, the way in which you fund needed social services, must be the paradigm for all economic exchanges.

Anyone who is involved in a market system understands that the primary dynamism of a market economy is not to collect and redistribute money, but to create money, and that this creation is a dynamic process that requires a whole series of practical virtues and insights and disciplines that very often are moral disciplines in themselves.

Now, how can we achieve a synthesis, or at least a dialogue, between these two mindsets for the betterment of our culture and for the betterment of our country? Well, I guess the place I'd like to begin—and here's where I state the thesis of this kinder, gentler libertarianism of which Ms. Marshall spoke a few moments ago—is to assert that there is a connection between theology and economics, on the level of Scripture, on the level of history, and on the level of practice, and that this connection needs to be appreciated by both social conservatives and by economic conservatives.

To understand the religious basis of the appreciation of an economic system, we need to go back to the book of Genesis and look at the very context in which the human family is created. In fact, even before the human family is created, we read on the first page of the Bible that God creates the heavens and the earth. That is to say, God makes the material world. In making the material world, he pronounces this material world to be good. Remember that, in Jewish and Christian theology, what is asserted here is the idea of theism, and not the idea of deism. That is to say, in the Jewish-Christian concept, the God who creates *ex nihilo,* from nothing, is the God who retains a connection to the creation. God may be found in the midst of His creation; God breaks forth from His creation, and there is no point in the material universe that cannot be the point of discovery of the occasion of the invitation to relationship with this God who made and sustains the universe.

The universe carries within itself and within its own nature the logic of its orientation and its proper end, which is God. Likewise the human person, we read in Genesis, is a composite that God forms from the dust of the earth and breathes into this dust the breath of life: corporeal-physical and spiritual-transcendent. The human person is both these things. Not spirit inside of flesh, but spirit and flesh. God seeks to permeate the whole entirety of who we are as human beings in our very nature. We can't get away from this reality. This is the Jewish-Christian presupposition of who the human person is. I know that sometimes there are tendencies and temptations to get away from this so that we become so heavenly minded we're no earthly good.

Also in the book of Genesis, we read that human beings, who are created in the image and likeness of God, are given a particular calling, a particular vocation, and it is the vocation to work. This vocation to work is not something that occurs as the result of sin, but it occurs before sin. In effect, what God calls the human race to is a collaboration with Him in the ongoing creation of the world.

This theological, Biblical understanding of who human beings are and what our context is in the midst of material scarcity, is the natural connection to what later comes to be known as economics. Because we are situated in the context of scarcity, we cannot have all things at all times. Some things are more abundant, and some things are more scarce than others. We must then begin to develop a way in which we live out this human reality, this existential reality, in a way that is appropriate to us as human beings created in the image and likeness of God. In the course of the centuries, this endeavor was undertaken. Most particularly it was engaged in about the middle of the 16th century among this group of disciples of St. Thomas Aquinas, who were moral theologians. This endeavor occurred in various places, but in particular it occurred in Salamanca, Spain.

These scholastic moral theologians began to raise questions about supply and demand, about the legitimate rate of taxation, about what the just prices of goods were, about the morality of inflationary policies on the part of the monarch, about the moral basis of the right to own property, to acquire property, and to trade property. All this moral, theological endeavor that begins and germinates in Salamanca is what Joseph Schumpeter, an Austrian economist who wrote the book *History of Economic Analysis,* called the beginnings of scientific economics.

I very often joke with my economist friends who may see me at a seminar on economics and say, well, it's good to have a priest in our professional setting. And I say, no, no, no, no, I want to welcome you to the discipline of moral theology, the sub-discipline of moral theology. There is, on the theological level—and indeed in the history of ideas, the historical level—an intricate connection between these two things.

There is also a practical connection, which we are called to confront today in the midst of a whole host of policy changes, and a different set of questions is being posed in the national dialogue. That is to understand first and foremost, that no economic transaction takes place outside of some kind of value consideration. It simply cannot be done. To the extent that anybody could even begin to approach such a practice, that is, just exchange without any kind of value or moral consideration, we end up in a very precarious situation where human beings become means to other people's ends.

Economists cannot pretend that market transactions take place in a moral vacuum. Likewise, believers cannot pretend that economic realities do not exist. Within the past few weeks, a statement was issued by the Wisconsin Council of Churches, bemoaning and deriding and attempting to slow down the welfare reform efforts of Governor Thompson in the state of Wisconsin. I read the Council's statement, and a line stood out. It said that "in the name of the poor" certain things needed to be done that were in effect non-negotiable. Then it said that it does not matter what it costs: these things must be done. This is a modern example of a misunderstanding—this heavenly-minded attitude where you're no earthly good—that can be very dangerous. To think that cost does not matter, that there's no moral responsibility, to consider the way in which we do things—I'm afraid of what that kind of thing leads to.

Let me draw some distinctions in terms of practice that may help offer a bridge between economic conservatives and cultural conservatives. The first distinction I'd like to make is that which was drawn by Robert Nesbit in a book a number of years ago called *Quest for Community.* In this book he draws the distinction between authority and power. Authority, he says, is a form of constraint like power. Unlike power, it is not a form of coercive constraint. Authority exists within a community and can constrict behavior in a wide variety of ways, yet does not resort to coercion in order to achieve its end. Power, on the other hand, is the direct hand of coercive initiation.

The point that Nesbit is making is that, when authority erodes, power needs to fill the vacuum. What I think we are confronted with in many areas, in the current debate, is precisely this erosion of authority. Authority, not just in terms of keeping families together and sanctioning immoral activity, but also in terms of the authority that requires and inspires of us action on behalf of those authentically vulnerable, authentically in need. To the extent that the church and the synagogue and other mediating institutions have been replaced by bureaucratic and political, i.e. coercive power, in meeting human needs, it is to that extent that the moral authority has been diminished in our communities.

Not many years ago, when I was growing up in Brooklyn, Mrs. Rabinowitz would sit atop her stoop and survey the neighborhood and all the kids playing in the neighborhood, and all she had to do was call your name out, and you froze in your tracks, because she'd tell your mother. My mother used to refer to Mrs. Rabinowitz as the mayor of the block. I told this story to other New Yorkers, and they said, yes, yes, we had one of those on our block: the lady who would sit there and watch, governing without government. I suggest that a great part of the tragedy of what is happening in our inner cities is the absence not of power, but of authority. To the extent that our mediating institutions can reconstitute themselves and gather this moral authority, and I know that's an intricate and complex process, but to the extent that we can do that, we need not resort to political power. We need not resort to bureaucratic rules of governments.

I would also like to offer a caution to those who prize freedom as the most important value. Freedom and human liberty is of course the context in which all virtue becomes possible. It is not itself a virtue. It is merely the context in which virtue can be realized. No one can perform an action that's virtuous or heroic unless that action is chosen freely. The opposite is the case, too. You cannot be named as guilty of something that you did not choose. Liberty is essential for virtue. God creates the world and gives us liberty, even the liberty, as Frank Meyer says, to damn ourselves. It is a mistake to think that this liberty is unanchored to anything else. Someone once said, "I love liberty more than the truth." If you disassociate liberty from the truth, you do not have libertarianism, you have libertinism. You have the erosion of all values that make civil society and human benevolence possible.

Liberty must be oriented to something beyond liberty. You cannot go through your whole life keeping all your options open, because, if you have done that, then you are not a human being. You have not made the commitments necessary to actuate the human potential. Liberty must be oriented to the truth, and to the truth of who the human person is in our totality. There is an inner logic in liberty that points beyond mere freedom. As the Holy Father recently said, quoting Lord Acton, though he didn't identify Acton, "It's not the liberty to do merely what you want to do, but the liberty to do what you ought to do."

I think there can be a great breadth of agreement between economic conservatives and cultural conservatives. Much of the area in which we can agree are the means to achieve the ends. Speaking as a conservative, traditional Roman Catholic, I think we can achieve a lot of the social agenda that we want to see for our country without using the political apparatus. There will be some instances in which we have to use government to protect the rights of people to their lives and to property and to other things in the civil order, especially in the midst of a period of transition where we're trying to enable the civic order, which has been for a variety of reasons frayed over these last 40 or 50 years, to re-cohere. I think that, in the midst of all of that, there can be a fruitful dialogue and indeed a collaboration to achieve similar ends between social conservatives and cultural conservatives.

Then finally, I would just like to close by making an observation about the obligation to the poor. From my religious tradition, this obligation to the authentically vulnerable, to the economically marginalized, is not something that I can dispense with. It is not just something that I can do if I feel like doing it or if I have a little bit of extra money; it is an integral part of who I am as a Christian believer.

First of all, so important is this obligation to minister to the needs of the vulnerable, that we in the first instance cannot surrender that task to bureaucrats and to the state. To the extent that we surrender that task to the state, even with the thought that somehow the state will advance our agenda, to the extent that we do that we abdicate our moral responsibility.

Second, we also turn over to the state the very occasion for the evangelization of our country. The church, in its removal from orphanages and from schools and from soup kitchens and from the multiplicity of other social service agencies, is also removed not just in the practical sense of feeding these people and reverencing the image of God in each human being, but we're also removed from the context of being able to love those people authentically and present the Gospel to them. We surrender the essence of what the Christian faith is about. In doing that, I'm not recommending that we coerce or make rice-Christians out of people, but merely to love them and to say, "Look at what motivates me to do this and see if it makes some sense for you."

Then finally, I think we need to take this commission so seriously that, rather than spending lobbyists' money and great effort and great time and great energy in bemoaning the proposed reforms, we instead begin methodically and systematically seeing in what ways we may be obligated to mortgage our churches and our lands and property, to cut salaries of our clergy, and in other ways make available the practical means for the amelioration of poverty—and not just by the transference of wealth. If we seriously begin to do this, we will seriously reevaluate many of our own programs and find that many of them have emulated government programs by being preoccupied with transfers of wealth, rather than with finding some creative way to see that, within the poor themselves, there can be a way in which they can lift their own lives, and that all we have to do is be there and support them in a way that has regard for their dignity.

If the principle of subsidiarity—the principle that says that human needs are best met at the most local level possible—were practiced, we would come to know the people to whom we minister in a way that would build a natural synthesis, and our cultural values could be applied and actuated within the communities in which we live, but we would also recognize the economic realities that we ignore only at our peril.

FURTHER REMARKS
IN RESPONSE TO QUESTIONS

Father Sirico

We will have accomplished nothing and maybe even gone back if all we do is replace a liberal welfare state with a conservative welfare state. Moreover, it is very dangerous if we begin to make churches basically contractees of the government, because down the line, what you end up doing is socializing the most effective sphere of private social service. Moreover, there are other ways. Dr. Novak earlier mentioned indirect ways of helping these communities. I think a system of tax credits, rather than tax subsidies, allows the money to be funneled through, and leaves the money in the community rather than just devolving it down through government. What could happen in the states is the same dynamic that has happened at the federal level. You can have the same distortions that go on in Washington going on in Lansing and in Albany and in all the state capitals as well. Rather than having money being taken up and then redistributed down, I would rather leave money down and earmark a certain liability for social spending, and then allow people to choose their priorities in their local communities.

David Frum

Conservatives fight these fights with one hand tied behind their back. There is now a very conservative judiciary. The Supreme Court in fact is not as conservative as the appellate courts are—in fact, when people complain about the fecklessness and lack of work ethic of the current president, that really is a mistake: President Clinton is far behind schedule on making appointments to the appellate courts, and I think we owe a great vote of thanks to his unwillingness to do a solid day's work. Still, those conservative judges follow an ethic of precedent that the liberal judges before them did not follow. That's how you get into this flag-burning mess. The Supreme Court's flag burning decision in 1989, outrageous though it is on its own terms, was in fact from a legal point of view quite a correct decision if you looked at how the courts had previously interpreted the First Amend-ment. It was very hard to see how, while respecting precedent, the Justices could have come out the other way. I think you're going to have a great deal of difficulty in liberating churches from the control of the state.

Now the one great advantage in the religion area, as opposed to the free speech area, is that the courts' precedents here are so chaotic that there are opportunities for creative judges to take one path rather than another out of the wilderness. For example, as I think many of you may know, while it is illegal for the state to supply church schools with textbooks, it is legal for the state to supply church schools with atlases. You find that, through the mess the courts have made in this area, there are opportunities if the right kind of judges want to take them. I think that you're going to find it's going to be very difficult, barring very large legal changes, for much in the way of government money to be delivered through religious institutions to poor people. If you want to use churches to deliver aid, you're going to have to reduce the role of government in providing the money in the first place.

Fr. Sirico

Let me amplify this last point. I think that one of the things to keep our eye on in this whole debate is the extent to which we have so politicized and socialized so many of these institutions that, whenever we're using direct tax moneys, an atheist, or a libertine, or a nihilist can object to chastity education in a public school. We have the situation now where, in the public school systems in some of our counties, you can distribute condoms to teenagers without parental consent, but you may not give New Testaments to children even with parental consent. The crux of that problem is the socialization of the education system.

The second problem that I think we need to keep our eye on is that he who eats the king's food sings the king's song. I don't know who said that, but if we're going to receive direct moneys from the government, then I think we have this problem with accountability. That accountability then impedes the insight and initiative and creativity of these institutions that have to deal with people on very individual levels. Sometimes somebody needs a good swift kick in the backside and sometimes they need a hug, and bureaucrats can't tell the difference because they have to fill in forms, and you can't do that on such an individual basis.I would relinquish the government's part of social services to the ACLU, and say, "That's fine, sure—but then don't tell private apartment house owners whom they can and can't rent to." If you want to create a moral atmosphere, allow moral sanctions to come into play in our localities and things like that. To the extent we depoliticize social services, we're going to have less of an argument with these people.

Then, finally, I think this is another argument for tax credits. You're not having the government subsidize organizations, you're merely saying, "Look, you have a tax liability for social service. You pay that tax liability through any one of a number of agencies that can be certified as serving people under the poverty level." I know that a strict libertarian is going to say, "No, we don't have any obligation like that at all." Well, that's fine, but that's not the world we're living in. The more people have the opportunity to direct their tax liability, the more they're going to become involved, and then maybe in the future we can have a society where that kind of liability does not have to be imposed by a governmental structure. Perhaps then we can have a society in which these social mechanisms are in place to offer other kinds of sanctions that are not political.

David Frum

We hear so many horror stories about government that one of the things that we tend to forget is that with the exception of a few disaster areas (the city government of Washington, D.C., for example), American government is, in general, run with a very high degree of professionalism and a very low degree of corruption. It will not be true that, if you move responsibilities outside government, other institutions will right away come anywhere close to matching either the general level of integrity or the general level of competence of government. This is one of the reasons that a past generation of reformers insisted on putting everything into government's hands: that the opportunities for professional management in government were so great. I think one of the things that people who want to reduce the role of government in society, because they are aware of the harm it does, have to be candid about, as the great Tocqueville was, is that localism and decentralization do mean a willingness to put up with a certain level of slap-dashness, a certain level of incompetence that is going to prevail because local institutions are not going to have anything like the professionalism of government.

Tocqueville made the observation that one of the things that happened in Europe was that Europeans became so intolerant and impatient of the mistakes they saw at the local level that they believed in centralizing everything. They saw the costs, but they were blind to the benefits. I think that is something that we are all going to have to make up our minds to—that there is a trade of short-term competence and efficiency for long-term benefit, for long-term self-government, long-term civic spirit, and— I believe, and I think Father Sirico will probably believe—the long-term betterment of the benefited parties themselves.

Fr. Sirico

What I would ask you to do is go back and talk to these kinds of people. Talk to agencies that are serving the poor in your community, and who also do not receive government money for doing that, and see what kind of response you get to this tax credit idea. Agencies that receive significant portions of their money from the government realize they have to reconfigure some of the ways in which they are doing things, and typical parish churches, who are not heavily invested in some type of project, may not have an insight. I think it's very sad that a number of national charities have said nothing on tax credits, but wring their hands about the cuts that they're going to face without realizing the potential that is out there. Then secondarily, I would say, it is a mistake for the church or mediating institutions to think that they have to replicate what the government does, that they have to raise the same amount of money and do the same kinds of programs. They can do it more creatively, more innovatively, and less expensively, because they are not supporting this massive bureaucracy that sits on these programs and that creates a political lobbying force. I think there's room for a new way of configuring the problem.

A number of years ago, a group called Abortion Rights Mobilization challenged the tax-exempt status of the Catholic Church because of our stand on abortion. I think that's a problem. Now let's keep in mind that we're talking about different things when we talk about a tax credit and a tax deduction, but there is a legal status that you have to have.

When I testified before the House Ways and Means Committee on welfare reform, Charlie Rangel, Democratic congressman from New York, said to me, "Father, you don't believe in government subsidy for religious groups?"

I said, "No."

He said, "But you're tax-exempt." The whole way of thinking there is that if you are tax-exempt, then you are subsidized.

My response was: "Well, Congressman, your confusion comes from the political presupposition that it's your money in the first place. I think it's the person's who produced it in the first place." We can educate people that it's not the politicians' money. It's your money in the first place, and you may have some responsibilities, but there are a whole variety of ways in which you can meet those responsibilities without having it filtered through the bureaucracy. Maybe we need to educate. Maybe that needs to be a piece of the whole political conversation. The right to private property—which has a social destination, I agree, but I think it's better achieved not through state apparatus but through the market system, which will meet social obligations to a greater extent than political institutions will.

David Frum

One of the things you do want to avoid when writing your tax laws is a lot of administrative complexity. I also think that we should not be utopian. I think of myself as a fairly radically mind-ed person, but we should not be utopian about the prospects of entirely eliminating government from the provision of the basic guarantee of subsistence. I think, since that isn't going to happen, since nobody really intends for it to happen, it's probably not a good thing to pretend that you are really trying to do it. The tax credit idea is a very interesting idea, and one I've been toying with, but I think that when you think about how it's going to work, a very high priority has to be minimizing the level of gov-ernment scrutiny of the organization, minimizing the opportuni-ties for political officials to send subtle signals about what they like and what they don't like.

If you're giving tax credits, then everybody who is eligible for a tax credit should get the same one. You shouldn't get plus points for having something be available to a locality; there shouldn't be more plus points for groups that promote adoption over abortion or abortion over adoption. Once you have decided that you want to reduce the role of government in the provision of social assistance, you really want to minimize the opportuni-ties for it to grow back.

Fr. Sirico

I concur with that, although I want to hold up a radical alter-native. The political reality, especially sitting in this city, seems to be that we must always think of the government as the resource to which we turn, and I want at least to propose the idea that we can change our thinking and think of the government as the resource of last resort, not the most desirable resort, but lit-erally the last resort. I want to propose that radical alternative to the way in which this city tends to think about these problems. I concur that, whatever we need to do on the level of prudence, it needs to be very clean and simple so that we don't complicate it and breed the kind of corruption and motivations that come from bureaucracy, which the Virginia school of public choice has tutored us in very well.

PANEL DISCUSSION: DESIGNING LEGISLATIVE MEASURES TO STRENGTHEN CIVIL INSTITUTIONS

Introduction

Jennifer E. Marshall

The next panel will look specifically at the problems and the possibilities of legislative measures to strengthen civil institutions.

Bill Mattox serves as Vice President for Policy at Family Research Council. He's a frequent speaker and a prolific writer whose work has appeared in the *Wall Street Journal, The Washington Post, The Washington Times, USA Today,* and numerous regional newspapers. In 1994, Mr. Mattox won the first prize in the Amy Foundation's Annual Writing Awards Contest. In addition to his writing, Mr. Mattox has testified before a number of Congressional committees, offered commentary on major television news programs, and served as project manager for two national public service advertising campaigns. This symposium would not have happened without his support.

William R. Mattox, Jr., *moderator,*
Vice President for Policy, Family Research Council

The role that I get to play now is that of moderator for our next panel, where, as Jennifer mentioned, we are going to be wrestling with questions about policy instruments specifically related to civil society and whether, in fact, government can play any role in promoting civil society or whether perhaps that is an oxymoron. Among the questions that we are going to be wrestling with are some that actually have emerged in the discussions from the earlier panels, questions like, "How do we avoid strangling faith-based institutions with regulations that may ultimately cause them to water down or abandon their distinctive faith-based quality?"

Other questions that will be discussed will be questions like "If we are to agree that tax-based measures are preferable to government contracting, how should the tax treatment of charity be structured?" and then "What sort of priorities should be given to changes in the tax treatment of charity, and for that matter, the tax treatment of marriage, and the tax treatment of child-rearing?" I'm thinking most especially of the flat tax, which as you know is gaining a great deal of momentum and enthusiasm. I think it'll be interesting for some of our panelists to consider how tax-based measures may be structured, as well as the priority that should be given to these instruments, *vis-à-vis* other tax initiatives out there.

We are going to kick things off with Michael Gerson, who is the policy director for Senator Dan Coats and a chief architect at the Project for American Renewal, which is a set of legislative proposals that Senator Coats has introduced in conjunction with Bill Bennett at Empower America. Mr. Gerson has also served as senior policy advisor to Jack Kemp at the Heritage Foundation and assistant to Charles Colson at Prison Fellowship. He's a well-known speechwriter and has done some exemplary work in this area, and I think he will be a great person to kick things off here in our panel discussion. Please join me in welcoming Mike today.

Michael Gerson, Policy Director, Office of Senator Coats

Several years ago at a New York news conference, Mother Teresa was asked by a reporter, "How do you change society?"

She responded with a question of her own, "How do you change society if you first don't bring individuals face-to-face with God?" I think that's an interesting question. I think it's a challenging question, and it forces us to go beyond the normal boundaries of our welfare debate.

That debate, it seems to me, is crippled by at least two false assumptions, even on the part of Republicans. First, we've focused almost entirely on the role and rules of government.

40

Second, many on both left and right seem to have a flawed account of human nature and human needs. The first assumption has led Republicans to claim too much for devolution to state governments, in my view. It serves a useful purpose, making power more diffuse and accountable and all those arguments. The primary problem with poor and suffering communities in America is not the level of government at which welfare spending takes place. It is the breakdown of institutions that create and transmit values: churches, neighborhoods, families, civic institutions. Respecting, restoring, and depending on these institutions is the hopeful frontier of welfare policy. I think many of you would agree with that.

The second assumption, a reductionist view of human nature, has also misdirected our welfare discussion. On the left, you find the materialism which is focused only on meeting physical needs through government. On the right you have a form of economic determinism which is focused only on changing the economic incentives of welfare with punishments and rewards. People are more than material, and more complicated than their incentives. They are moral and spiritual; their needs are complex, and their problems, in many cases, are only solved by efforts that both feed the body and touch the soul. This role is beyond government at every level: federal and state. It is played by private and faith-based charities armed with tough love and true compassion.

Government may have lost the war on poverty, but that war is being won every single day in communities around the country. It is our theory that creatively empowering these charities, expanding their resources and role, is the most promising, exciting trend in welfare reform. With these goals in mind, Sen-ator Coats and Bill Bennett have brainstormed on some practical ways to begin shifting resources in America from government towards these institutions. We need to be bolder than we have been in the past. The goal is not just welfare reform, but welfare replacement—giving compassion back to the private sector.

The result of this thinking is the Project for American Renewal, a package of 19 bills. It is organized around three goals: giving power and resources to families, giving power and resources to private grassroots community organizations, and giving power and resources to private and faith-based charities. We have described this as a more radical form of devolution, not just to state governments, but beyond government entirely. We want to privatize welfare, not because we're stingy, but because only these institutions of civil society hold real hope for those in need.

In this effort, as we've alluded to, we need to be very careful, and we've tried to be. Government help can bring government rules. Charities that are dependent on government often sacrifice their central spiritual mission. This is the reason our plan has avoided direct government grants to religious institutions. We have included vouchers, which seem to present far fewer problems, and we have proposed changes in the tax code, which I think is the cleanest approach of all. The centerpiece of the package is a charity tax credit, which will allow individuals to give $500 of what they owe each year in taxes directly to private charities in their own communities. The measure would shift about eight percent of total welfare spending, about 100 billion dollars over five years, directly to faith-based institutions combating poverty, without government interference, and without government strings. I think this would be good public policy, exponentially increasing the effectiveness of this funding.

I want to close with a political and moral point. I think that Republicans and conservatives have sometimes fundamentally misunderstood the nature of Christian political involvement. Grover Norquist refers to evangelicals as part of the "Leave Us Alone Coalition," along with gun owners. There is an assumption that an anti-government message is sufficient to appeal to this group. If this is accurate, it is profoundly disturbing. I don't believe it is accurate. The Christian tradition is not "leave us alone"; it is love thy neighbor. All of us are justifiably skeptical of government, but none of us wants to be guilty of abandoning the ideal of compassion. It is essential that we craft policies that encompass both this skepticism and this moral commitment.

I believe those policies should nurture effective private efforts, institutions that shape our character and direct our lives. I believe these proposals can and should capture the moral imagination of Christian conservatives. They understand, after all, that the public interest depends on private character. They understand that the common good requires that goodness be common. They realize, that, if we want to change our society, we must first bring individuals face to face with God.

William R. Mattox, Jr.

Peter Ferrara is the General Counsel and Chief Economist at Americans for Tax Reform. He has served as Senior Fellow at the National Center for Policy Analysis, at the Heritage Foundation, and at the Cato Institute. Mr. Ferrara has also served as Associate Deputy Attorney General in the U.S. Department of Justice, a senior staff member in the Office of Policy Development in the Reagan White House, and a special assistant in the U.S. Department of Housing and Urban Development. Please join me in welcoming Peter Ferrara to our panel.

Peter Ferrara, Chief Economist, Americans for Tax Reform

Why would we want to privatize the welfare state? Well, first of all, the current welfare system is just such an incalculable disaster that I don't need to belabor that too much. The point is made by this simple fact: We spend over 350 billion dollars in America today on almost 80 welfare programs at the federal, state and local levels. That's a record by any measure, and it's substantially more than we spend on national defense. We spend 20 or 30 percent more in America on welfare than we do on national defense, and yet the poverty rate today is about the same as it was in 1966 when the war on poverty started. It's 14.5 now; it was 14.7 then. It was 15.1 last year. In spite of all that expenditure of funds, we don't seem to have made much progress. As Robert Rector has ably pointed out in many of his publications, in many ways, we're worse off because the poor suffer from a spiritual poverty today that was not in existence in times past.

I believe the welfare system itself is responsible for this, because the welfare system that has been built by the state rewards counterproductive behavior and penalizes productive behavior. If you don't work, then you are qualified for all these programs. If you follow a policy of non-work, which will lead you to poverty inevitably, you are rewarded. If you go to work, then they take away all these benefits, so you're penalized. If you have a child outside of marriage, you are rewarded with all these wonderful programs that they give you to help you. If you marry somebody, particularly someone who works, well, that's it. They take them all away, and they walk out and you're on your own. They penalize you. Now, lo and behold, if you look at the statistics from the mid-1960s to today, you find an enormous collapse in work effort among the lowest income groups of the population, and you find an enormous increase in births outside of marriage. The proof is in the pudding.

Well, why would you want to privatize it? Why can't we just have these government reformers come in and re-do it? Well, first of all, we know they can't do it. They've been promising to do it over and over again. We did a paper at the National Center for Policy Analysis in which we first advanced the tax credit idea that I'll describe in a moment. In that paper, we argued that the private sector was more effective at welfare, at delivering welfare assistance. First of all, we showed that they're more efficient and more effective. If you're in trouble in America today, you're far more likely to get help right away from a private-sector group than the government. If you go and apply to the government, you could drop dead before they give you any assistance. Where you get the assistance immediately is from the private-sector groups, and they're far more effective at getting you off assistance once you're on. Unlike the government, they don't keep you on till past the time you're dead. The government still sends out checks to Social Security recipients who have long since passed away. The private sector has proven far more effective at moving people off welfare more quickly.

It's much more than that, and it's really the points that Mr. Gerson was talking about earlier. The private sector is able to impose moral requirements that the government is no longer capable of imposing. In the private charities, they say, "If we're going to assist you, you have to get your act together. You have to get educated. You have to stop taking drugs. You have to stop getting drunk every day. You have to go to work. You have to stop having children outside of marriage," etc., etc. Our government has proven entirely incapable of imposing these kinds of moral requirements.

I think there's something more fundamental here about why you have this result in the private sector and not in the public sector. That is because the private groups are voluntary organizations. They depend for their existence on support and agreement from their local citizens. That means they better reflect the values of the people—because they have to be consistent with those values in order to get the support voluntarily that they need to keep them alive. With government bureaucracy, as you know, if you don't want to pay them what they demand from you, they have ways of forcing you to do so. They don't really care whether they're consistent with your values or not.

What we proposed in terms of privatizing welfare is the Taxpayer Choice Tax Credit. The way that would work is: Every individual in America would get a tax credit for contributions to private 501(c)(3) groups focused on assisting the poor. You have to be focused on assisting the poor to be eligible for this credit. People would be allowed to give up to some limit. It could be $500. We originally proposed a proportion of your taxes that's equivalent to what the government spends on welfare, as the ultimate model.

Suppose you give $500 to a local homeless shelter which you think is far more effective at helping the poor than some of these state government programs. You take that $500 off your federal income taxes, so you're completely reimbursed. The federal government then takes that $500 out of the welfare block grant for your state. The federal government doesn't lose anything on that.

What is the end result of this? You've created competition between the public sector and the private sector. Now the public sector has to compete to keep those funds against the private sector. That is likely to improve the performance of the public sector as well as of the private sector. More fundamentally than that, you've shifted the power over the entire system to the tax-payers themselves. They now decide who is doing a better job. Is it the private groups, or is it the governor of their state? That's why we call it a taxpayer choice. We believe that ultimately what will happen is that you will shift the control of welfare to the private sector to the extent that taxpayers support it.

Now, anything to do with the government will never work perfectly, so there are a lot of areas where this can be entirely messed up. One was raised before. How do you determine which groups are eligible for this tax credit? We propose to try and take advantage of the current 501(c)(3) system, where people apply to the IRS for 501(c)(3) status, which has worked fairly well. We would have an additional form that you would staple to your application, that you want "501(c)(3) plus" status, so you can be eligible for this credit. In that form you would indicate that you are going to focus your assistance on low-income people, and what your basic methodology will be. You would want them to follow a policy of easy approval, as they do for 501(c)(3)s today. They won't spend a lot of time calling you up and investigating you. The idea is to let the taxpayers do the investigating, in effect. The government can always mess this up, but, if you do this right, the system is very workable.

Now let me just suggest a couple of modifications for this that could be pursued at the state and local levels. Let me draw an example from my own experience. In Fairfax County, Virginia, we have this awful, awful tax, which should have been abolished a long time ago, called the personal property tax. It's this huge tax they put on your cars, and nobody can ever afford to pay it, because they assess it all at once annually, and you end up paying more in personal property taxes than you paid for the car by the time you're done. Suppose we said that, if you took on a personal responsibility for someone in need, we would waive the personal property tax for you that year. Most people pay from $500 to $1500, depending on the value of their cars. Suppose you took in a homeless person and took on the responsibility of helping him get his life back together; then we would waive the personal property tax for you. Suppose you took in a single mother with a child, and you took the responsibility for supporting them and trying to help them get their life together; then we would wave the personal property tax for you.

Both these proposals, the tax credit and this one here, follow the philosophy of Marvin Olasky, which indicates that what's really effective is focusing one-on-one with people, instead of these big government bureaucracies.

William R. Mattox, Jr.

John P. Walters is president of the New Citizenship Project, an organization created to advance a renewal of American institutions and greater citizen control over our national life. He served as Deputy Director in the Office of National Drug Control Policy during the Bush Administration and was an assistant to Bill Bennett at the U.S. Department of Education between 1985 and 1988. During 1993, he was a visiting fellow at the Hudson Institute. Please join me in welcoming John Walters to our discussion.

John P. Walters, President, New Citizenship Project

In my five to seven minutes, I'm going to try to make certain points that I think are somewhat at odds with some of the things that have been said before. First, we need to be clear about the issue we're trying to get at, and that is a fundamental institutional failure. Not just failure of welfare institutions, but also of educational institutions, and—particularly for the most disadvantaged young children—of law enforcement. There are even failures down the line that people are aware of, even though there's some unwillingness to discuss them frankly, in institutions like Social Security and Medicare. There are concerns about private institutions, such as marriage and the family, and about the normalizing of immorality in the arts, entertainment, political leadership, and even, in some cases, in religious leadership.

In the face of that kind of institutional failure, private and public, there is now a working consensus that part of this decay is what some have called a moral poverty. Fixing this is not a problem of simply reforming bureaucratic structures, whether inside or outside of government, but of addressing moral poverty in the institutions of society.

In terms of governmental reform, the narrower topic of this panel, a new division of labor has to be established. There has been a tendency to pull authority into large bureaucratic structures that are intentionally not concerned with morality, that in fact are antithetical to moral concerns, and that are supported by a whole body of theory and training in contemporary social work, contemporary psychology, and contemporary political and social thought that doesn't take the moral dimension seriously. If you're going to overcome that, you have to rely on institutions that use moral standards.

The issue then is how to devolve both resources and power to a new institutional structure. The precondition is the division of labor. We ought to, (1), say, "There are things that government at various levels can't do and that you as an individual are responsible for, or you as a community are responsible for," and, (2), be clear about what state government is responsible for and what federal government is responsible for. Right now, everybody, especially the federal government, is kind of responsible for everything, and that means nobody's responsible for anything in particular, and so accountability is diminished.

As Aristotle said, you need not only virtue but also the equipment for virtue, and I think that means not only money but also a look at such coercive things as social stigma and law enforcement, and you need to be clear about how you're going to use those.

As for federal tax credits, generally speaking, I'm opposed to these for the same reason that I am opposed to long-term block granting. If you really want to have a debate about what society wants, cut the federal government. I would urge a reform agenda that calls for cutting local and state government bureaucracies as well, and returning the debate from the federal level to the states, not only by cutting programs but also by cutting taxes and restoring the tax base to citizens, who can then consent to the programs they want. Use the moral capital of the American people, who are already concerned about the direction their institutions are going, to give guidance. You don't need to get into a kind of new bureaucracy or a new set of regulations for local programs.

My penultimate point is to focus on the middle class. I think that the tendency to focus on the most disadvantaged, as a social welfare state does, has weakened the middle class, which is the source of capital. The government is taking authority and resources from the middle class. You can draw on middle-class values like individualism to help foster individual responsibility and self-government, and you can push those forces against the culture of victimization and the nanny state.

Lastly, we need to be modest. I believe that, no matter what happens, there will be more inequality; maybe not grossly more, but, if you're going to allow people to make a difference through their own responsibility in their communities and their lives, there's going to be a difference depending on what they do, and you have to be willing to indulge that and not try to buffer it with the bureaucratic state, which in any case doesn't really redress inequality but makes a promise to do so that tends to make people think it's doing so.

You have to have basic accountability in the institutions that remain. The division of labor ought to make institutions responsible: city councils, police departments, educational systems, and those that help the disadvantaged. We ought not to promise secular perfection the way the welfare state and the liberals have. There will probably always be poverty because there will be kinds of personal behavior that foster self-destruction, and we ought to be candid about that. There's a tendency now to be less than candid with the American people, and to make them think we can create a private welfare state that will do what the public welfare state didn't do. I don't believe that's possible. I think that it's possible to have improvement, but I also think it's unrealistic to expect that, when you devolve the welfare state back to the private sector, you're going to do it by telling the American people they're all going to become private-sector social workers. Most members of the middle class whom I see in my personal life would like to have more time and resources to spend with their own families, with their own churches and in their own communities. I think tax cuts would increase the amount of time and resources people have for those things, but I don't think you should promise excessive increase in community involvement because I don't think it's going to happen.

We must be willing to tell the disadvantaged the same things we tell the middle class, that ultimately they have to rely on their immediate friends and family and their community and, most of all, themselves, and not make people think that they can always count on a governmental hand, whether it's a conservative or a liberal one. It's a fine line here between loving your neighbor and being cold-hearted. In our political and social environment, one of the most profound disservices we do for the disadvantaged is make them believe that they can and should count on somebody else to fix problems or to buffer the effects of self-destructive behavior. I think a core part of the message has to be frank, and it's not going to be particularly welcomed, especially by liberal elites. The communities that are making a difference to the most disadvantaged are taking that message to heart.

The national discussion ought to include what I would somewhat glibly call show trials, continually hammering on the failures of the bureaucratic state and the successes of places that are succeeding. Right now, we are in a very dubious discussion about a seven-year balanced budget which, however important it is, is not the end of reform. I am concerned that the real ends of reform will not be nearly as prominent as they should be in a presidential debate.

William R. Mattox, Jr.

Last, we're going to hear from one of my favorite people in Washington, Robert Rector, who is Senior Policy Analyst for Welfare and Family Issues at the Heritage Foundation. Robert testifies regularly before Congress and played a key role in developing the welfare reform proposal that the House Republicans included in their Contract With America. Mr. Rector's articles on welfare and family issues have appeared in *Policy Review, National Review, The American Enterprise, The Journal of Labor Research, The Harvard Journal of Legislation, The World and I, Human Events,* and other publications. He's also co-editor of *Steering the Elephant: How Washington Works,* a book analyzing the internal management of the Reagan presidency. Please join me in welcoming Robert Rector.

Robert Rector, *Senior Policy Analyst, The Heritage Foundation*

Let me say to start off that I support the tax credit proposals that have been talked about here today by Peter Ferrara and Mike Gerson. I think that those are fine proposals if only for the point that they get money away from the government, which I think is a wonderful thing. I think the less money that flows into government welfare programs, the better off the poor will be. I do think that they have certain limitations, and we need to examine and think about those limitations as a way of enhancing these proposals rather than belittling them.

The first limitation I would point out is that, even if we put these proposals into effect, most of the government welfare state will continue. It will continue to reward people for dysfunctional behavior and for destroying their lives, and we will be spending something to the tune of two trillion dollars through government welfare over the next five years to do that. In a certain respect, one image I have of these proposals is that, as a tidal wave of destruction moves towards our society, we give the private charities a box of Band-Aids and go out and say, "Here, stop it." There are limitations. As long as the government is pushing very strongly in one direction, there's a limit to what private charity can do to stop the disintegration. In particular, the out-of-wedlock birth rate is rising at one percentage point a year. I don't see anything in these proposals that would stop that. If it's not stopped, I think everything else is largely irrelevant.

Second point: even if we have a tax credit policy like this, we need to recognize, as Marvin Olasky has pointed out, that most existing private charity out there that exists today is abominable.

Most private charity has completely subscribed to the same ethos that undergirds the public-sector welfare system. I could call that ethos *therapeutic permissiveness*. If you doubt me on this, just go to a conference of welfare providers run by United Way and you will find virtually no difference between United Way and HUD. Even if we have a system in which a tax credit allows funding to come out of HUD and into United Way, which I think would be good, I would still estimate that probably 90 percent of the funds would be used in a counterproductive manner.

The third and, I think, most important point I would make is what I call the Humpty-Dumpty scenario. I'm a very simplistic thinker, and I have always felt that you have two approaches to a problem. One is to wait for Humpty Dumpty to fall off the wall; then you come around with some scotch tape and glue, and you try to put Humpty back together again, which is basically what the social welfare system does. You have a woman who was abused as a child; she's an alcoholic; she's had three children out of wedlock before she's 22; she's been on AFDC for four years; now she's homeless. Well, let's fix this, okay? There you are with your glue and your scotch tape. You're trying to put families with multiple, overlapping dysfunctions back together again. In my view, the best thing is probably not to push Humpty Dumpty off the wall in the first place. You can probably get more bang for the buck if Humpty stays on the wall than if you try to tape him back together again after he's busted into a thousand pieces.

That brings me back to my central image of what civil society is and what civil institutions are and the role that they should play in the overall transformation of our society. As I go back and look at Tocqueville's original depiction of civil institutions in our society, I see that he essentially was recognizing that these institutions are what we could call *value-generating institutions*. Value-generating institutions, institutions that generate the habits of the heart and the habits of virtue within each of us, that allow us to live next to our neighbors without murdering them, that allow us to be parents, that allow us to become married and stay in the discipline of marriage, that make civilized life possible, are essentially operating like a social immune system. He didn't have those words at that time, but, essentially, when you look at Tocqueville, that's exactly what he's saying. These value-generating institutions are an immune system. They are what keeps Humpty Dumpty on the wall in the first place.

When I look around at the inner cities of the United States today, I see one institution that is spectacularly effective in combating the collapse of marriage, in combating poverty, in combating crime—and it's not midnight basketball. It is, of course, the church. If you go inside an inner city today or even look across our country in general, you will find that young men who regularly attend church are 50 percent less likely to become engaged in criminal activity and 50 percent less likely to become engaged in drug abuse. Young women who regularly attend church are also 50 percent less likely to have children out of wedlock. These institutions are tremendously effective in shaping the hearts and minds of people to immunize these young people against the assault of culture on their values, against all the temptations to self-destructive behavior that both the secular culture and the government offer them.

The question that we have here is, "How can we best institute policy changes that mobilize and unleash these civil institutions, the churches in our communities?" It's very important to have tax credits that would allow them to engage in social work, to replace government social work and so forth, but I think there's a much more powerful mechanism for doing that—for going to Humpty before he falls off the wall rather than trying to tape Humpty back together again when he's landed on the floor. That change is very simple. What I would like to see as a complement to the tax credits that are being talked about here is a model program in which we would take existing federal education spending for low-income people, convert it into a model school-choice program, then take ten communities around the United States, and in each of those communities guarantee to each poor parent a voucher using combined local, state and federal funds, a voucher equivalent to what that parent would have spent on her child in the public schools. In D.C., that would be around $11,000 a year. I'd like each parent in D.C., in Detroit, in Chicago, if she's low-income, to have a voucher of $11,000 a year and to be able to take that voucher to any school of her choice. Back to the public school if she's so foolish, or to a private secular school, or to an overtly religious sectarian school. Any school of her choice.

I had an experience about one month after the last Los Angeles riots in the early '90s. A group of black pastors came into my office, and they wanted me to be a liaison with HUD and with Secretary Kemp. They wanted to get some kind of funding to set up a tire-recycling plant in Watts. They were going to take old tires and turn them into asphalt and so forth. I looked at that, and I said to them, "Gentlemen, I really don't know that much about your capacity to run a tire-recycling plant—I frankly think it's probably not too great—but I do have a tremendous confidence in your capacity to do what your primary function is as pastors, which is to shape the hearts and minds of the next generation of young people." Then I threw them this voucher plan. I said, "If we had a voucher in Watts, such that each of your parishioners could get $9,000 per child and could use that $9,000 for education in any school that he chose, how many of you as pastors would open up a school as an adjunct of your church?" Of course, every single one in the room said he would—*overnight.*

I would emphasize that schools are very low-capital institutions. You can literally open a school up in a few months. All you need is an empty room and some desks. A teacher is the harder part to find, but those too are available. As well as seeing civic institutions strengthened by way of the type of tax credit that we have talked about here today, I'd like to complement that with a model school-choice system in which, in certain selected cities, every poor parent would have these federal funds available in a voucher that she could use in religious institutions for the education of her children.

If we did that, what we would see within a single year is dozens upon dozens of religious schools opening up in our inner cities, all adjuncts for churches in those communities. Each of those schools would not only be a moral haven for the children in it, but also a moral beacon reaching out into the larger community. I think that's a very important point, because, going back to my image of the tidal wave and the Band-Aids, what we clearly need in all these communities, and not just in the inner city, but across our country, is a pervasive change in our moral culture.

As long as the moral culture is drifting one way, it's not going to help us that much to be out there trying to pick up the pieces in a few religiously based drug re-hab programs. Those will be great programs, but again, they're going to be overwhelmed by the negative forces arrayed against them. What we need in the inner city is a pervasive change in the culture, change in the values that are given to young people. I think that the only way to accomplish that is to get education—which is primarily a function of shaping the hearts and minds of young people, of shaping the habits of virtue of the next generation—out of the secular monopoly and turn it over to the civil institution primarily equipped to do it. I think that we in fact can do this. I'm very encouraged by some of the remarks that we're beginning to hear from the left and a softening-up on these issues, and I look forward to seeing the types of tax credits that are being talked about here today complemented with this sort of religious school choice option.

FURTHER REMARKS

William R. Mattox, Jr.
Let me ask your reaction to Bill Bennett's recent remark that, while in his view the two are not mutually exclusive, a charitable tax deduction or credit is actually in his mind a higher priority than a flat tax.

Michael Gerson
Senator Coats has a simple and fairly politic answer: he's a supporter of a modified flat tax. I think there's good evidence that

there is a relationship between the tax treatment of charitable giving and the level of charitable giving. I believe getting rid of the deduction would in fact be a form of social engineering that would be very disturbing. I would also associate myself with Dr. Bennett's comments, that our goal is not always in these circumstances to increase the economic rationality of our economic system. I've had people tell me that they oppose the child deduction because it subsidizes a form of consumption —children—as though they were the same as BMWs. I think that we need to reject that, and I think that the Congress is likely to reject those kinds of approaches.

Peter Ferrara

We at Americans for Tax Reform are working for a flat tax, and I was one of the authors who developed the idea of the tax credit. That indicates that I don't think that there's a conflict between the two. The reason there's not a conflict is that the tax credit is just a form of giving you your money back, allowing you to shift the government's money from the public sector to the private sector. It is not a way of having you reduce your tax burden. You are just shifting welfare funds from the public sector to the private sector. It is really a welfare initiative, a taxpayer choice initiative. It's not inconsistent with the policy behind a flat tax, which is that the tax system should be neutral as to these different systems and should focus on having the lowest rate possible and on most efficiently raising the amount of revenue that has to be raised. There is no inconsistency between the two ideas. A tax credit doesn't violate the tax policy behind a flat tax.

As for a charitable contribution, let me just say two things about that. First of all, we did a big experiment in the 1980s as to the impact of the charitable contribution on the tax code. What that experiment indicated was that it doesn't have a big effect. They lowered the rates dramatically during the 1980s from 70 percent in 1980 to 28 percent by 1990. What that did was lower the value of the charitable deduction because it was worth 70 cents on the dollar at the beginning of the decade and it was only worth 28 cents on the dollar at the end of the decade. What happened to charitable contributions during the 1980s? They soared. Charitable contributions soared during the 1980s. Part of the explanation for that is that most people who can make charitable contributions don't take the charitable deduction. It only applies if you itemize, and only a minority of people itemize. In addition, most of us who are promoting the flat tax are perfectly willing to go along with the provision that says we'll have a home mortgage interest deduction and we'll have a charitable contribution deduction. The important thing behind a flat tax is that you have a single flat rate, and you get rid of the loopholes that allow some people to avoid their tax liability so that they're not paying their fair share. Those are the two principles. You ought to be imposing equal obligations on people. If everyone pays the same rate, then you pay the same proportion of your income as everyone else. Those are the critical elements behind the flat tax; otherwise, this is a very compromisable issue.

John P. Walters

It's not whether or not there's a deduction; it's whether or not people feel they have the resources to make additional charitable contributions. That's why I think tax cuts are a crucial part of enabling people. A growing economy in the '80s allowed greater charitable giving, as well as a climate in society that encouraged this as a moral and private decision. In terms of the credit and shifting money, I really would like to hear how you avoid bureaucratizing the eligibility issue such that even private institutions have the same problems as *bureaucratic welfare states.* Look at the United Way, for example: A number of agencies that are now recipients are social action groups of one kind or another, and not really classic, community chest organizations. The kinds of organizations that are likely to be national and be able to qualify and be able to advertise and be able to attract that kind of giving may not be simply the ones that we're looking for when we talk about dealing with social problems through the private sector. How you administer eligibility may determine whether you create a kind of private welfare state that really doesn't do what you want to do.

William R. Mattox, Jr.

Let me add one item as well, Peter, that I'd be interested in hearing you respond to. In a tax credit situation where you're offered a trade-off between a credit or sending your tax dollars on to the government for various poverty-fighting programs, how do you avoid the kind of problem that Robert Rector was talking about where you tend to favor approaches that wait for Humpty to fall off, approaches that are remedial in nature, rather than provide equal incentive for people to give to more preventive sorts of programs, like church-based institutions that may in the long run do more to, say, reduce the problem of out-of-wedlock pregnancy?

Peter Ferrara

There is no way to deal with these government programs that's invulnerable to difficulties. A lot of conservatives have criticized school vouchers because they say they're likely to lead to the government controlling private schools, and the answer is that that *is* a risk, but it's a risk you have to take because you've got to reform the current public school system. I think this is an analogous risk. The government could make a mess out of this idea in how they qualify people to be eligible for these credits. We have outlined a system that has been embodied in legislation and seems to be workable, and I discussed it briefly in my remarks. The idea is to build off the current 501(c)(3) process. That process has worked well. They could mess it up in the future, but it has worked well in the past because they have not gotten into the substance of what you're for or what you're against when you apply for 501(c)(3) status. They just look to see that in fact they are going to be devoted to helping low-income people, and apart from that they don't get involved in making a decision as to whether they like the way they're helping low-income people or not, because the taxpayers are going to make that choice.

You don't need national groups to do this. Local groups who want to form a 501(c)(3) to help out the homeless don't need to be national. They send their application in, and they become a 501(c)(3), and they help out the homeless, and they are just a local group. Small groups have a better opportunity to get tax credit funds from their neighbors, under this kind of system, than they do to get a federal government grant. That's when you really need to be a big, sophisticated national group and you've got to hire your lobbyists and your lawyers and everybody else and you've got to send your representatives to Washington and talk to people and get the grant. The little local group, that religious-based group that's helping the homeless, is not going to be able to do that. This gives them opportunities to go to people in their local community who are right there and say to them, "Look, you can give us money that otherwise is going to go to the federal government, and it doesn't even come out of your own pocket." They can make their case one-on-one.

As to the point that Robert Rector raised and you mentioned, these groups would not be based on a Humpty Dumpty approach at all. The taxpayers would decide what kind of groups should get the support under this kind of system. Robert makes a good point. This Humpty Dumpty approach is not really the way to solve this problem in the long run. You have to stop people from falling off the wall in the first place. Presumably, taxpayers would find that argument appealing. It would focus their contributions on groups that are effective in stopping people from falling off the wall in the first place. Now I wouldn't want to ignore the people who have fallen off, so I would want to give some money to help the people who have fallen off, but I would want to give money to groups that are focused on stopping people from falling off in the first place.

I don't agree that most of the governmental welfare state would continue under this. If they did this the way I would do it, I think taxpayers would privatize the whole thing. Every time you give people a choice to get out of a government mess, as they did for example in Chile with Social Security, 90 percent of the people get out. I think that's what's going to happen. If you did this the way it's been advocated, 90 percent of the welfare state would be moved to the private sector.

I have to confess that my concern is not the proliferation of non-profits. There is a valid concern that you don't want groups getting into non-profit activities as a sham and then taking a lot of property out of the tax base when in fact it's not being used for non-profit purposes, thus creating an increased burden on people who pay property taxes (which I would abolish, by the way). There are lots of ways to control that. I would oppose a general crusade to stop the proliferation of non-profits.

Robert Rector

I would add that HUD isn't contributing to your tax base either and the public sector is not contributing anything to your tax base. If the essence of this reform is to move money out of the public sector and into the non-profit/private sector, then there isn't going to be any net loss to your tax base because the government is a tax-eater, not a tax-builder.

Michael Gerson

On this question of the presence of non-profits in a community: when you look at some of the social capital studies that John DiIulio talks about, you see that, if you're trying to predict community failure and if you're trying to associate it with the presence of certain institutions, the number one institution is retail liquor stores. If you're trying to predict community success, the number one indicator of success is the presence of a church. I think there's obviously a tie between the community and the non-profit structures. The stronger those structures are, the healthier a community is.

Peter Ferrara

Robert Rector's proposal on vouchers is a very good one. I would also suggest that something like that can be done at the state level, that you don't have to wait for the federal government. You could set up a voucher program at the state level saying we're going to give 10,000 or 15,000 vouchers to low-income people. That is a way to get the whole school choice thing moving, to start working from the bottom up. Focus the proposal on low-income people in the inner cities. Those are the ones who are worried about school choice. Then over time you expand it to more and more groups because, once everyone making below $15-20,000 has the right to school choice, then everyone making $20-30,000 is going to say, "What about us?" and everyone making $30-40,000 is going to say, "What about us?" and that's how you're going to get the thing going.

Michael Gerson

We do have a pretty ambitious school choice component in what we're trying to do. I want to say in addition that I don't think it's a simple division between federal and state, particularly on that issue. We represent a very conservative state, yet the education lobby in that state is more powerful than at the federal level by far. I think it's a question of picking our fights on some of these questions. I don't think that vouchers would have much of a chance in Indiana at all. Just as a kind of note of realism, I think feeding that kind of reform in inner-city situations through federal approaches is not necessarily without some merit.

Robert Rector

The Milwaukee school choice program has been in existence for a couple of years now, but there are only a few hundred vouchers, and in the most recent wave of that they were trying to get the vouchers to be usable in religious schools, and that went to court, and I'm not sure what happened. Maybe someone else in the room knows. I would make one point on that. It shows exactly why you need to have a pervasive change. I think it's great that that program exists in Milwaukee but if you look at Milwaukee, has anything really improved there? You've got to have a massive change. This is not something where you're going to tinker around the edges and achieve social redemption. What is needed in Milwaukee is a full-scale voucher program where instead of a $1,000, which I think is what their voucher is worth, they get $8-9,000, what is currently being spent on each child. Let everybody in the country come in and compete for those funds, and then I think you might begin to see a turning of the climate. It won't be easy to turn around a society that is on a downhill Alpine slope. It is very steep, and tinkering is not going to stop the avalanche of social disintegration.

John P. Walters

The other area where there's a fight going on right now, as I understand it, is in the 1996 D.C. appropriations bill, because the Speaker has apparently dug in his heels on whether or not there's going to be a voucher plan in that bill. In this case, although I spend a lot of time criticizing federal activity, as I read the Constitution, the federal government is responsible for the District of Columbia. I think that in the voucher battle it's important to break the back of the unions and the bureaucratic monopoly. There's an important battle going on in Milwaukee, and I think there can be an important battle going on in D.C., which is why this is such an issue. This may get lost here in Washington in the next couple of weeks, but it shouldn't. Because if you make it stick here, you begin to show the difference and you begin to see that there's a challenge to a failed urban public school system. I know every big city thinks their school system is the worst, but it's hard to break this because the people who generally vote, the middle class, already exercise choice. They move or they turn to private schools, because no rational person is going to say, "I'm going to run for school board, change the whole school system in order to fix this." I'd rather go out and take a second job and pay for private tuition. The voucher fight is one of breaking down an established force against this kind of change, and I think this is one case where a little battle in a couple of prominent places really can have a watershed effect. That's why in fact the union is going nuts trying to crush every single effort in the most brutal and all-out fashion everywhere, because they know it's a glass house and, if you start breaking things, a lot of breakage will happen quickly.

William R. Mattox, Jr.
Thank you very much for a very interesting discussion.

LUNCHEON ADDRESS

Introduction

Jennifer E. Marshall
Dr. Marvin Olasky is Senior Fellow at The Progress and Freedom Foundation, where he is studying the most effective methods for assisting the truly needy and designing replacements for the current welfare state. He is the co-founder of the Center for Effective Compassion, inspired by his landmark work in the study of charity, *The Tragedy of American Compassion*. He is currently writing a sequel, *The Promise of American Compassion*. Dr. Olasky is editor of *World* Magazine. He is also professor of journalism at the University of Texas at Austin and the author of nine books on history and cultural analysis. He has co-authored six other books as well as numerous articles for publication such as *National Review, Policy Review, Christianity Today,* and the *Wall Street Journal.*

Of all the speakers here today, Dr. Olasky is probably the one who needs the least introduction. His work has dramatically redefined the terms of the national welfare debate, and he is an excellent choice for a transition from the morning to the afternoon because he has reformed the debate precisely by focusing on the names and the faces of the people who are doing the work at the grassroots. He has made our national debate much richer. Please join me in welcoming Dr. Marvin Olasky.

CHARITABLE EFFORTS TO REPLACE THE WELFARE STATE

Marvin Olasky, author, The Tragedy of American Compassion, and co-founder, the Center for Effective Compassion

As I look around the room today, I see so many people from whom I've learned so much and whom I honor: John Perkins, who's been doing wonderful things for 30 years; Wayne Gordon with the Christian Community Development Association; Guy Condon with CareNet; Duane Higgins from Alabama; Rev. Ron Moore from Mississippi; Father Sirico; Bill Schambra from the Bradley Foundation; Rev. John Woods and Mrs. Woods here from the Gospel Mission here in Washington. It just goes on and on.

What can I possibly do to explain what's going on to all these folks whom I esteem, people from whom I've learned so much?

A few thoughts—and this may not be always the best organized speech you've heard this year, but it comes from the heart. I start out by thinking about all the people here who are not only well-intentioned but also intent on seeing good results, who understand the difference between effective compassion and what is well-intentioned but often does exactly the opposite of what it sets out to do. I've found in traveling around the country this year lots and lots of soft hearts, wonderfully soft hearts, but alas, they tend to go along with soft heads.

You see this in church bulletins with notices about helping the homeless. Here are three that have been brought to my attention this year. First, "Thursday Night: Dinner for the homeless. Medication to follow." Here's another, "At the evening service tonight, the sermon topic will be 'Seeing Hell Close Up.' Come early to meet homeless visitors." And one more, "Don't let homelessness kill you. Let the church help." A lot of good intentions, a lot of soft hearts, some soft heads as well.

This is a wonderful hotel to be meeting in [the Willard Hotel in Washington, D.C.]. This is the hotel where U.S. Grant used to hang out when he came here right after the Civil War, or as we call it in Texas still, the "War of Northern Aggression." U.S. Grant, when he stayed here following the Civil War, did not have much of a sense of humor. You could excuse him for that. He had seen too much during that terrible war in which 600,000 soldiers died. Recently, I visited the Cold Harbor Battlefield, southeast of Richmond. That's the one where Grant ordered three frontal assaults against strong Confederate positions. It was obvious to the soldiers that they could not make it. It was so obvious that they sewed their names and addresses to the backs of their uniforms before the battle so that their bodies could be identified and the next of kin notified more easily. Grant later said that his biggest regret of the whole war was ordering that third charge. The first, maybe, just to see whether it could be done. The second, dubious. The third, just a total tragic disaster. They had no way of doing it; the body count just went on and on.

At least U.S. Grant admitted that he had made a mistake. That is far more than some liberal defenders of the welfare *status quo* are now doing. *The Washington Post* yesterday had a headline, "Daschle Says Final Welfare Plan Has Lost Democratic Support." All that's left apparently is to defend the *status quo*. That should be an oxymoron: a liberal defender of the *status quo*. That's a combination that's not quite right, like dry rain or trustworthy Clinton. Alas, the liberals, who come from such a proud tradition of looking at the horizon, going where no man has gone before, or at any rate no sane man—liberals, with this wonderful tradition of so much progress, particularly in racial matters in this country—are now left with defending the *status quo*. How the mighty have fallen.

It's even worse. We saw through the '70s and the '80s how children suffered as families dissolved, or never were formed, by people who had the consciousness of the '60s. Some had soft hearts, but many had soft heads. Now in the '90s, the last refuge of liberalism, with its great tradition, is to defend the *status quo* and to push forward the children again as hostages. The body count of those children over the last 30 years is enormous. They're stacked up like soldiers were at Cold Harbor. To go at it again is a third charge at Cold Harbor. At least the folks who defend the *status quo* could have the decency to sew the name tags on the backs of those children.

As you can see, I'm not fond of what passes for the Democratic position these days, but I can only give one or two cheers for the Republican position, because conservatives have not really taken advantage so far of the opportunities to replace welfare that have been created by the failure of liberalism. Many conservatives are still content to be the party of hard-headedness and, in perception and sometimes in reality, of hard-heartedness as well. They tend to say, "Okay, we're hard. We have hard heads. Maybe we have hard hearts, but you folks on the other side have soft heads and soft hearts, and when it comes right down to it the voters will prefer hard-hard to soft-soft." Well, maybe they're right politically. I think not. I don't think they'll be successful in retaining public confidence long enough to end the budget deficit if they do not deal with the compassion deficit. That's something the Republicans have not really dealt with yet for the most part. Maybe they can get away with hard-hard versus soft-soft politically, but what's right and what the American people want are folks who are warm-hearted but tough-minded. People want that combination, and so far neither party has really been producing it as its main position.

Conservatives need to realize that cost is not the main reason at all to fight governmental welfare programs. It's a factor, certainly. It becomes a huge tax burden for middle-class taxpayers. The real fundamental problem is that we're too stingy in what's truly important: treating people as human beings made in God's image, not as animals to be fed, caged, and occasionally petted.

The real need is for leaders who are tough-minded, but also tender-hearted and willing to recognize the creation of people in God's image and the need to treat people in that way and not just looking at it through green eye-shades as a budgetary matter.

There are some conservatives who have realized that. There are some who understand that. Newt Gingrich does. He's getting terrible press these days. He's gotten hard press all year, but he understands this. Bill Bennett understands this. There are some senators, Dan Coats, John Ashcroft, Rick Santorum, who understand this. There are some members of Congress and some governors I've met in my travels around the country this year: George Allen, Kirk Fordice, Fife Symington, John Engler. I think they have a sense of this, and it's starting to come out in the way they speak. It's starting to come out in the types of legislation that they are moving through their states. The critical understanding here is that private programs that are challenging, personal and spiritual can do a better job than these failed governmental programs and that people who are really concerned with helping the poor, with protecting children, should not be going any more for this failed *status quo.*

Until that becomes the common understanding and message, until liberals are ready to move away from the *status quo,* until conservatives are ready to understand that it's not primarily a budgetary matter, that it's a matter of dreams and not just dollars, then poor people will stay on the welfare plantation, and folks who want to misuse the word *compassion* to derive political capital will still get away with it.

When you get around the country, when you get outside Washington, there's absolutely no reason to be in social or political despair. Why? Because both history and the present-day efforts represented by many people here in this room show us the alternative to either soft-headedness or hard-heartedness. That's what I want to emphasize right now: the positive alternatives, the way good things can come out of this year's effort despite the failure of both political parties to approach this question adequately.

Let me just mention quickly the history, and what it shows. After all, the reason I'm speaking to you today is that I spent a year in the bowels of the Library of Congress searching through old records and I became a witness to what the predecessors of many folks here in this room accomplished. I can testify to all these folks whom the standard history books have forgotten. If you had history courses in high school or college, I suspect you've never heard of some of these people whom I'll just refer to today; there are lots more who are great heroes of faith in practice.

Men like Charles Brace. Here's a guy who, over a 40-year period, from 1850 to 1890, built lodging homes in New York City that provided shelter to several hundred thousand abandoned children and then over the years placed 91,000 children in adoptive homes. This was his life. This was his career. This was his calling and he performed it wonderfully.

Women like Helen Mercy Woods. From 1881 to 1903, she ran a shelter in Chicago for pregnant and unmarried women. Month after month, she gave personal attention to each newcomer. She rejoiced as their babies were born. She helped some of her charges get married, others to place their children for adoption, some to get jobs. She kept at it year after year as many people in this room have kept at it year after year.

I can testify about some other forgotten heroes and heroines. Annie Richardson Kennedy ran a home for unwed moms in New York City between 1900 and 1920. Her goal was to first bring the girls in touch with their Savior and then build character. She provided love and opportunity for thousands, and then she disappeared into the fog of history. My wife doesn't mind when I fall in love with women like Helen Mercy Woods or Annie Richardson Kennedy; they've all been dead for a long time. The textbooks are silent; they've been forgotten. I want to testify to the contributions they made. They're part of a larger story that none of us learned about in high school or college or wherever.

During the 19th century, before the feds ever got involved, there was a war on poverty that, considering the degree of difficulty they had, considering that America was a much poorer nation a hundred years ago than it is today, was far, far more successful than ours. It was a war waged by tens of thousands of local, private charitable agencies and religious groups around the country. It was successful not in that they abolished poverty, but in that they witnessed movement out of poverty by millions of people. It was successful because there were springs of fresh water flowing among the poor, not just blocks of ice sitting in a perpetual winter of multi-generational welfare dependency, always winter and never Christmas. It was successful because the optimism that was prevalent then contrasts so sharply with the demoralization among the poor and the cynicism among the better off that's so common now.

I can testify that there was a great cloud of witnesses to effective poverty-fighting. They succeeded in large ways by knowing and doing small but vital things. They knew first of all that the literal meaning of compassion is not writing a check, but having personal involvement with the needy, suffering with them. That's what it means: com-passion—with-suffering. Suffering with them, not just giving to them. They knew that welfare doesn't mean passing a bill but helping a person fare well. These are some simple, elementary things that our legislators seem to have forgotten. The older generation knew that people should be challenged. When an able-bodied man, for example, came to a homeless shelter, he often was asked to chop wood for an hour or two. Maybe whitewash the wall of a building. That way, he could provide part of his own support and also help those unable to chop. They knew. They taught it through those work tests that even the most run-down person is not just a taker; he can also be a giver. They knew that everyone is made in God's image and is capable of helping.

Why have so many people forgotten that? Well, we don't know much about history. They taught us what to avoid. They warned us. I'll just give you a few of their warnings, which are amazingly prophetic. Mary Richmond, one of my heroines from the Baltimore Charity Organizing Society in 1897, said, "Relief given without reference to friends and neighbors is accompanied by moral loss. Poor neighborhoods are doomed to grow poorer whenever the natural ties of neighborliness are weakened by well-meant but unintelligent interference."

Carl Herrick is here from the Daylight Foundation in Louisiana, where he is trying to get some good stuff going. Well, the New Orleans Charity Organization Society in 1899 wisely noted: "Intelligent giving and intelligent withholding are alike to charity. Giving money to a poor person by itself is morally neutral. The action can hurt if not done wisely. If done well with discernment, it's the best thing in the world. If done poorly, you're only helping a person continue on the path of destruction."

New York Charity leader Josephine Lowel: "The problem before those who'd be charitable is not how to deal with the given number of the poor; it's how to help those who are poor without adding to their numbers and constantly increasing the evils they seek to cure."

They were very forceful. One of them said: "It's important to reform those mild, well-meaning, tender-hearted, sweet-voiced criminals who insist upon indulging in indiscriminate charity." They were prophetic, but we don't know much about history. We've forgotten America's past successes in poverty-fighting, and the result has been the waste of not just billions of dollars each year but the death of part of the American dream.

Now let me take a moment to mention something that some members of Congress understand very well—but others need to drop the green eye-shades and get into real people, real lives, real dreams, and not just the dollars. The essential problem of the welfare system now is that sometimes it succeeds in keeping people fed but it kills dreams. It kills the helping dream of many Americans. You know, most of you, millions of other people would like to be generous at the entrance to the Metro here in Washington or at street corners in your own towns. But if you know—and there have been studies showing this—that most homeless recipients will use any available funds for drugs or alcohol, the tendency is to end up walking by, avoiding eye contact, and there's a subtle hardening that occurs once more.

Welfare kills the dreams of social workers. A lot of conservatives sometimes talk as if social workers are our enemies. Not so at all. These are extraordinarily, for the most part, well-intentioned people. The common lament they have is, "All we have time to do is move paper." Here's a comment from a young social worker who had the calling, who wanted to do it, worked at it for a couple of years, and then just couldn't do it anymore. He said,

"I had a calling. It was that simple. I wanted to help." Then he resigned. Frustrated and worn down, burnt out, realizing he just wasn't doing any good.

Welfare kills dreams among poor individuals who gradually become used to dependency. The worst thing for kids is the fatalism that often sets in. There are studies showing that, after a generation or especially two generations of welfare, there's a sense of "Whatever I do, it's not going to do any good. My mom was this way. I'm going to be this way. Probably my children are going to be this way." It just goes on and on and on—a form of fatalism.

Children need challenge. Kids need a sense of opportunity. They don't get that in the welfare system. In fact, they see that adults who sacrifice leisure time in order to remain independent, to work hard, are often called chumps rather than champs. It kills the dreams among children who grow up without fathers. Those of you who have coached Little League teams, if there have been kids without fathers there, you know. You know who's in that situation. They alternately cling and show stand-off-ishness in a way that kids with functioning dads don't. It breaks your heart.

Welfare kills. A couple of weeks ago, I spent some time in south central Los Angeles talking with some welfare moms there who told me about—here's an expression I didn't know before—*county check pillow pimps*. That's the expression they use. Guys who come in on the last day of the month. They're called county checks because in California you get the welfare check through the county. Guys come in on the last day of the month; they spend the night, and they get part of the welfare check that comes from the county the next day.

Welfare has deprived kids of fathers; it has deprived women of husbands. I'm not saying it's the cause, but it certainly is an enabler. Instead of helping ennoble people in poverty, helping them fight, welfare tells people to give in. It enables them to stay in it. It kills.

It packs a theological as well as a cultural punch. After all, how do children understand the nature of God the Father? How do wives understand that Christ is the Good Husband for His bride the church when they have no experience at all with good fathers or good husbands and they don't know anyone who has in their whole block?

Washington conservatives need to spend more time with folks, with poor people who are striving to get out of welfare. If more people actually walked the mean streets a little bit, they'd come to understand this crucial point: The reason to fight these governmental welfare programs is not that they're too expensive, but that they're inevitably too stingy in what's truly important—treating people as human beings made in God's image, not as animals.

There is no reason to despair, because there is good news around the country. Folks here in this room who are doing it know it. We are recovering the lost tools of charitable success. We're seeing a new great cloud of witnesses emerge. We're living in an era with many heroes, or, I should say, ordinary people who become heroic as they show through hard suffering that the American dream of compassion is not dead.

There are people I've met who, when they started out in their ministries, were really folks whom you would not consider to be charismatic individuals at all. They've become so over the years. They've learned. They've grown.

One example—a friend of mine now, Bob Coté in Denver. He's a tall, white ex-boxer. He spent a year on the streets as an alcoholic in the early '80s; then he pulled together a few of his fellow winos and junkies to start a homeless shelter, a program in Denver that's become known as Step 13. Bob showed me his four-story building—and he'd be glad to give you a tour if you're in Denver sometime—how mostly-dead people from off the streets can step-by-step come back to life. They can get jobs with increasing responsibility. They can get rooms within that building that gradually reflect greater independence. They go from a big dormitory to kind of an alcove to a separate room with a lock on the door, and they're buying their own furniture and getting their own phone accounts, and they're ready to step out and lead independent, responsible lives. It's a tough, time-intensive process, but Bob Coté has been there himself. He's there to help others.

A person right here in Washington, Hannah Hawkins, lives down in Anacostia. She's a great person to visit. She's short, black and retired, but she voluntarily runs an after-school program that has several dozen children doing their homework, receiving the love they often don't get at home. You go down there and sometimes it's wild. Sometimes those kids run around like lost sheep, but she knows each one of her lambs by name. It's challenging; it's personal; it's spiritual.

I wish you'd come with me and visit Freddy Garcia in San Antonio. He's a soft-hearted but hard-headed Hispanic ex-addict. He formed Victory Outreach some 30 years ago in San Antonio to help substance abusers. Groups based on his teaching now have spread throughout Texas to California, even as far south as Peru. I've sat in his home this year. I've watched the way he patiently counsels and teaches those whom everyone else has abandoned.

This has been a good year for me with all the travel and hubbub and so forth. I've really been blessed to see and come to know some of these people. I'm here to testify that they succeeded, and they're still succeeding, and others can too. They have the common understanding—they picked it up somewhere, somehow—that compassion to be effective needs to be challenging, personal and spiritual, CPS for short. Just like CPR can bring back to life a dying person, CPS—challenging, personal, spiritual—can bring back to life that dying American dream.

Again, if you're not familiar with some of these places, go and visit. Go down about a mile to Clean and Sober Streets here in Washington or the Gospel Mission with Reverend Woods. At Clean and Sober Streets, it's interesting that there are really tough rules, as at the Gospel Mission. One strike, you're out.

There's compassion that's challenging, personal, and spiritual at the Right Alternative Center in Milwaukee. This is something that Bill Schambra from the Bradley Foundation knows about well, and has helped quite a bit. People sometimes say that AFDC moms will be stuck on the government rolls for a lifetime. The moms there have a 13-part pledge. They pledge to change their own behavior. Not to swear, not to shack up, not to do drugs. The leaders there challenge them to stick to their pledges. When they do, their lives change. Some of them get married, some of them get jobs. They run their households better. Their kids start doing better in school; the kids break out of their fatalism. That's the key enemy, not poverty, but fatalism.

There's compassion of that sort, from what I've read, at the Union Gospel Mission in Portland; the Disabled Businesspersons Association in San Diego; the Resources, Inc., program in Brooklyn: those are the Samaritan Award winners this year. You'll be hearing more about them later. I've read their reports: challenging, personal, spiritual. Not easy. Not easy at all, but possible.

I've personally seen some successes over the years. I've seen lives of pregnant, unmarried women turned around. I've seen abandoned children happily adopted. I've also seen failures. Recently, I was working with a homeless ex-con. I thought he was making good progress, but now he's slipped back into irresponsibility. He's in jail now. He's having a hearing next week. Maybe he'll get out and have another start. I sent him over to the most challenging shelter in Austin, Texas, the same day I sent my oldest son to college. My homeless friend Fred lasted just three days at the shelter, and then he went back out on the streets and is now in jail. My son is still at the University of Texas. It's not easy, but it's possible.

People do change. God changed me. He moved me out of the Marxism that I adhered to 25 years ago. He brought me to a knowledge of Christ. I'm thankful to Him. Other people can change. You see it all the time, and there's lots of experience in this room saying that.

In order to have confidence that this change can occur, we have to do a couple of things. They're not primarily political. The first thing we have to do is just awaken ourselves theologically in terms of putting God's principles to work. Then, only after that, do we have to start working on some public policy matters.

There are a lot of false Gospels that are being offered now. There are those in the religious left who say that the Bible mandates government transfers of resources to the poor on the grounds of, for example, Jesus' statement, "Whatever you did to the least of these brethren, you did to Me." Now I take that verse very seriously. Before we blindly use it to justify the welfare state, we need to ask, who are the "least of these" in America? What kind of help is real help? Certainly, children threatened with death before birth by abortion are among the least of these, and I would love for all of the groups in the Christian left that have been proclaiming so vociferously their love for the unwanted, the poor, and the neglected to work hard on abortion. Women abandoned by their husbands and children who grow up without fathers also have it very rough, and the concern should be how to give them hope, how to help them break out of that fatalism.

What about able-bodied homeless men? One of the prime changes in the welfare legislation that is chugging through Congress, surely to hit President Clinton's desk, involves trying to cut down, actually a real cut, on some aid to homeless men who are addicts or alcoholics. Here's a hard case, something that I think obviously should be changed. Does irresponsibility qualify a person for the ranks of the "least of these"? Jesus does not include in his list of commended charitable acts, "When I was strung out, you gave me dope." If we take seriously Christ's words in Matthew 25, "Whatever you did to the least of these my brethren, you did to me," then giving money that goes for drugs is akin to sticking heroin into Jesus' veins. Rather than proclaiming the dire effect of cuts generally, instead of proclaiming a fight to the death in defense of the *status quo,* like at Cold Harbor, why not accurately and carefully look at some of these measures, and say, "This is something that really *should* be cut."

Instead, we're just hearing the blanket condemnations of any movement away from the *status quo,* as if any change at all is an indication of hard-heartedness.

If we straighten out the theology, the practice follows. When I was a Marxist, I believed in top-down approaches, emphasizing government redistribution. As a Christian, I now understand that change comes one by one from the inside out. Straighten out the theology of those who are rich, and there will be a tremendous expansion of effective compassion. Straighten out the theology of those who are economically poor because of poor values, and their attitudes and behaviors will change, and they will make progress. The essence here is revival and reformation among both rich and poor. That will transform American poverty-fighting. There would be such an outpouring of private charity, if we had that revival and reformation, that governmental programs could rapidly be replaced by private efforts, and we would not have to debate the question of tax credits.

While we can hope and pray for revival and reformation, it's not something that we can count on, so we come to questions of public policy. A firm distinction needs to be made—again fairly elementary, but I just don't hear it made—between providing and promoting. The Constitution talks about providing for the common defense, but promoting the general welfare. There's such a huge difference between, say, renting a hall for a convention, and manning every booth in that hall yourself. That's the difference between providing and promoting. We're in the mess we're in right now because the government has attempted to provide welfare, and instead it's given us entitlements and bureaucracy. There's a legitimate role for government in promoting the general welfare, but not in providing it.

That's where we come to this question of tax credits on either a state or national level. Frankly, I'd rather see it done on a state-by-state level, because we don't know exactly what the best tax credit mechanism is, or the best way both to promote discerning giving on the part of individuals and to avoid government entanglement as much as possible with religious and other charities. For example, we don't know whether a 100 percent tax credit is absolutely the best thing or whether a 90 percent tax credit would generate just about the same amount of income for private and church charities while requiring considerably more discernment on the part of givers because, let's say, on $1,000 they'd be putting up a $100 of their own money, and they might think a little more seriously about where it's going.

I am worried about the direct mail problem with tax credits, if it's no cost at all to the individual taxpayer. I do want to have some cost there. I'm also worried about credits without any personal involvement. It would be much better if we can work this out to have a situation where individuals receive tax credits and they also spend some time at the charities to which they are giving. The bookkeeping in that may be too complicated.

Tax credits, I think, are a very good idea, and I think the constitutional question of interference with religious groups can be worked out. If you have a coalition strong enough to get tax credits, you have a coalition strong enough to protect religious groups from federal interference.

It would be interesting to see if we could try some experiments on the state level. If we can't do that, and it may be very difficult to do that, then certainly going on a national level is something we need to do. There's no reason, in fact, why you can't have a national approach and state approaches at the same time, trying out different things over these next few years to see what will best promote community-based, poverty-fighting charities.

What I don't understand—and I'm hoping that people from some of the big charities will explain this—is why some of the big philanthropic and charitable groups are not really getting on the team for tax-credit measures. You'd think that they would be eager for such a reform, or else they're just in the position of saying, "No, no, no" to any change, more and more vehemently. I'd challenge those big charities. Why don't they propose something positive instead of defending to the death a failed *status quo*? If their concern is adequate funding for poverty programs, why not tax credits? Are they more concerned about the poor, or about holding on to their own power? I'm not sure. Everyone I've met from those organizations is well-intentioned, but it seems they've gotten used to kissing up to government officials instead of going to taxpayers individually and making the case to them that they deserve support. Well, I don't know, but it's a problem. It's a sad state of affairs.

There are people who say this just would not work. I was reading the other day about the case of a student of management named Fred Smith, who went on to found Federal Express. He described, in a term paper, his idea for a reliable overnight delivery service. His professor gave him a C and explained that the concept was interesting and well-formed, but, in order to earn better than a C, the idea must be feasible.

Charity tax credit proposals are feasible. We need to experiment a little bit, but we need to fight for them. We need to push the big philanthropies and the big philanthropic trade organizations, like Independent Sector and the Council on Foundations, to support them also.

While this public policy stuff is important, the tendency, especially here in Washington, is to fall into the trap of thinking that a particular piece of legislation is the solution. Charity tax credits are a great mechanism to take money off the governmental superstructure and stick it back on the bottom in private and religious charities where it can do the most good, but they're still just a mechanism. The more time I spend in Washington, the more I feel as if I'm reading from a manual for medical emergencies put together by people whose goals exceed their wisdom. It's like a recommendation from a student in a junior high school science class for a nose bleed: Put the nose much lower than the body until the heart stops.

The public policy change is essential, but we can't wait for that. You know the answer to this question very well, because you've lived it. The question is: How does each of us individually help children and adults now, one by one? How, in doing so, do we create models for the way the entire welfare system can be transformed and replaced? What first steps can those of us in this room take?

Especially in this group, I'm nervous about mentioning any of the things that my wife and I have been involved in, but they've been educational for us. Again, as a number of you who know me know, I am not always the most diplomatic person around. I want to be kind of a hard-nosed editor at times and so am not the nicest guy around. My wife is a much better person than I am in those ways, but I tend to think, "Okay, if I with my bullheadedness occasionally have been able with my wife to give a room in our home to needy individuals, to coach kids in baseball and tutor kids, and to mentor some folks, if I, not a particularly hospitable individual, a guy who would rather spend time in the bowels of the Library of Congress than actually helping someone directly, if I, once in a while, can do something a little bit decent, why can't people with much greater merits, with much greater abilities and niceness and goodness, do the same or even much more?"

I know that many of you already give of yourselves a lot. Can you do even more? Again, some of you I know are just working already to the max. Some of you have probably not been involved with the poor at all. Will you take a first step? Just think for a moment. If I were a liberal, I would want you to close your eyes and visualize world peace. As it is, I do want you to visualize, in your mind's eye, even with eyes open, one poor person that you have directly, personally helped during the past year. A lot of you, I'm sure can do that and can probably do that with lots and lots of people you can visualize. If you don't see anyone, I pray that you'll take a small step during the coming year, and maybe then even a larger one, tutoring a child for one hour a week, being a Big Brother or Big Sister, or Little League coach, mentoring an adult who's gotten in trouble, providing Biblical counsel to a young, unmarried pregnant woman, maybe giving her a room in your home, maybe adopting a child.

Those steps are hard, but we're surrounded. We are just so surrounded by a great cloud of witnesses, men and women like ourselves who have taken first steps and then many more. This is what I've learned mostly going around the country this year. Then remember chapters 11 and 12 of Hebrews, talking about the great cloud of witnesses. "Therefore, since we are surrounded by a great cloud of witnesses, let us lay aside every weight. Let us run with patience the race that is set before us." (Heb. 12:1)

Let's work theologically; let's work politically; let's work personally. As we work and pray, let's remember that 2,000 years ago Jesus Christ came into the world to suffer with us, to die for us, and in this year of our Lord it is such a great blessing to see godly people who follow in his steps.

It was six years ago that I began trying in my own real small way to resurrect the word *compassion* among conservatives and to promote some compassionate alternatives to failed welfare programs. I gave a talk six years ago at the Heritage Foundation, and I just ran across it in my files a couple of days ago while thinking about what I would say here today. I gave it at the time when I was in the middle of my historical research at the Library of Congress. Let me just read the ending of that talk:

"It's beginning to look a lot like Christmas. A time when God came to earth to teach, to suffer, and to save by suffering. A generation ago, Whittaker Chambers wrote, 'Suffering is at the heart of every living faith. That is why a man can scarcely call himself a Christian for whom the crucifixion is not a daily suffering.' Chambers knew that Christianity is based on suffering, I'd say 'suffering with,' but he recognized that the meaning of the faith 'has been blurred as Christianity, in common with the voices of a new age, seeks new escapes from the problem of suffering. Nothing is more characteristic of this age than its obsession with an avoidance of suffering.' Are we in America, and conservatives especially, serious people? Frankly, I do not know always whether I am. I do not know whether you are. I hope we are. I pray that we are, but I do not know. I do not know, but finding out is the challenge of the 1990s for the conservative movement."

Well, that was what I was saying in 1989. Now it's 1995. We've made some progress. The battle for the word *compassion,* the understanding of *compassion,* is now on. But the body count is growing. Those bodies that are Cold Harbors all over the inner cities of this country are just piling up. The defenders of this *status quo* are tenacious. At least we're in the fight. It's hard, but it's glorious. I've been glad to be fighting along side a lot of you this year. I pray that will continue and that we will overcome with God's grace. Thank you very much.

PRIVATE SECTOR COMMUNITY DEVELOPMENT: CREATING THE MEANS

MODEL PROGRAMS

Introduction

Jennifer E. Marshall

The next segment of the program really belongs to the Acton Institute. This is the segment in which humanity really comes to the fore, and I very much appreciate the Acton Institute's interest in using this as a forum for presenting their 1995 Good Samaritan Awards. I'm going to turn the podium over at this point to Kris Mauren, who's the Executive Director of the Acton Institute, and to Father Sirico, who's the president of the Acton Institute and spoke earlier this morning, and they will present the Good Samaritan Awards to the three finalists.

Father Robert Sirico

My earlier remarks were predicated on the Biblical vision of the obligation of charity. Another paradigm which could express that notion is the incarnation, Christ becoming flesh. He became like us in all things but sin. There's often a temptation, in talking about the philosophy and the grand ideas and even the nitty-gritty policy stuff, to forget that there are real people in real towns and localities who are doing real work and doing it effectively, so, last year, we put together the Samaritan Awards. The basic thrust is to display and to call attention to people who are effectively working without government assistance, without government oversight and regulation in their own communities, to reverence the creativity and the dignity of people who are in need. The three honorees do this in a variety of ways with some real innovation. I think you'll be very impressed. To explain these awards a little further, I've asked Kris Mauren, who's the executive director of the Institute, to give you an overarching idea of what it is, why we chose whom we chose, and also to give you a look at what we're going to be doing next year with this award.

PRESENTATION OF SAMARITAN AWARDS

Kris Mauren, *Executive Director, The Acton Institute*

It was a year ago that we launched the Samaritan Awards as part of several programs associated with the Institute's welfare reform initiatives for 1995. The first program we did was a national conference here in Washington last March, where we brought together theoreticians, social workers, academics, politicians, and others concerned about the well-being of our fellow man and talked about what a new vision for welfare would be like.

The second part of our major initiative this year was the Samaritan Awards, which was to put into practice and to honor in practice what we talked about at that conference. The first thing we did was invite nominations and applications from around the country, and, because we believe that the most effective and compassionate welfare system that we could have is a private one and one divorced from government influence, we asked that our applicants themselves be free from direct government funding. The nominations were widespread, covering every different kind of social-service activity you could imagine, and we had more than 700 applications over a three-month period. The applications included a mission statement, financial information, success stories, references, and a narrative essay responding to a series of questions which allowed us and the judges an opportunity to evaluate the effectiveness and replicability of their program in communities around the country.

Over a period of three or four months, we went through the process of reading and investigating the 700 applications. This was done internally by our staff. We sent people to go out and visit different charities around the country to see whether they matched the applications that we were so impressed with and how they did it. Indeed, we weren't disappointed by any of our visitations. This process was very time-intensive and often agonizing as we tried to whittle 700 wonderful organizations down to ten honorees.

Each of the ten Samaritan Award Winners received a $1,000 grant from the Acton Institute about two months ago. Those ten were also eligible to submit a more extensive evaluation to receive one of three $10,000 cash grants as determined by a national panel, and in a few minutes we'll be presenting those cash grants. In your registration packet today you received a press release about the Samaritan Award program, and on the back page it indicates the ten Samaritan Award winners this year with the three on the top being the ones who will be presented $10,000 checks today. You will notice down below, of the seven Samaritan Award winners at the bottom of the page, one is the Haven Drug Rehabilitation Program of the Gospel Mission of Washington, D.C., and I'd like to recognize at this time Rev. Woods who is with us and congratulate him and have you join me in congratulating him for being one of ten winners.

This brings me finally to today where we're going to be awarding these grants, but first I have some acknowledgments for which I'd like to ask your indulgence. The first is one of the readers in our office all last summer. We had three full-time people doing initial readings of applications and applying discernment on categorization, etc., of the different charity awards. One of those persons is with us today. Susan Mueller, a graduate student from Regent. Could you stand up, Susan? Finally, the Samaritan Award Program was funded this year by the generous support of primarily four foundations. They included the Scaife Family Foundation, the JM Foundation, the Claude Lamb Charitable Trust, and the Bradley Foundation in Milwaukee. I'm pleased today that we have representatives from both the Claude Lamb Charitable Trust and the Bradley Foundation, and I'd ask if you'd both stand up and be recognized.

Finally, I'm going to ask one by one the three recipients of the cash grants to come up and to be recognized and to speak to you for a couple of minutes about what it is they do and perhaps about the secrets of their success. The first one I'd like to present is to the Disabled Businesspersons Association, founded and directed by Urban Miyares.

Urban Miyares, *Disabled Businesspersons Association*
Thank you, Kris. Thank you, Father. They told me I only had two or three minutes. Usually it takes a two-day workshop to explain what I do. It took me two minutes to get up here.

The Disabled Businesspersons Association is really about you. After the conference, what happens if you get into a car accident, become a quadriplegic, lose your sight? Let's say you're diagnosed with MS, muscular dystrophy, cancer, or a heart condition. What are you going to do? What about your job right now? How would you be able to perform that job? You say, "Well if I do become disabled, I'll go to rehabilitation, get education, and learn how to do my job again." Well, the largest segment of the society today of unemployed individuals is people with disabilities. Three out of four people who are willing and able to work but have disabilities are unemployed. If you own your own business and you become disabled, which is the situation of a large segment of the people that we will deal with, how are you now going to run your business? Running a business with a disability is completely different from running a business without a disability. If you don't know what you're going to do, you'll do what most people with disabilities do—take the easy way out: quit and go on a welfare program.

What the Disabled Businesspersons Association does, since 1985, is provide free services to anybody with a disability who has that enterprising spirit or is already in business. We help with legal matters, accounting, and marketing. We help them do financing. Last year, we were involved with over 500 loan packages to banks. In 1995, we provided services to 3,572 individuals. We are now the largest organization in the world of professionals and business owners with disabilities. We do this with an all-volunteer staff of successful business owners who dedicate their time to help others.

The whole thing started 28 years ago when I came back from Vietnam as a disabled veteran. I was written off as unemployable. Multi-disabled, I was told I was not suitable for employment. As a matter of fact, they gave me 20 years left to live. I did what I wanted to do, and that was start my own business. I had a family, and I had to support it. I've been very lucky in business.

In 1985, when I owned a manufacturing company, a few disabled veterans I knew asked me to help them with their business, and that's how this whole thing started. By 1989, when I sold my manufacturing company, I decided this is what I wanted to do for the rest of my life. That's what we do now. We're expanding into other countries. We've been invited by Russia, Australia, and Taiwan to visit them and help their disabled become productive members of society.

So the Disabled Businesspersons Association is an information source, an inspirational source. We're an organization that helps people with disabilities get the right information on how to compete in the non-disabled world, because as a group, people with disabilities are not considered the same as minorities, so we don't qualify for programs other groups may qualify for. It's a rough road starting a business today, let alone to have a disability, but each year we help start over 800 businesses.

I can't tell you how many thousands of businesses we work with on an ongoing basis and how many businesses that would have failed if it wasn't for our involvement. The number one reason for business failure in America today—business failure meaning having to close owing others money—is disability. The number two reason is death. Not financial reverses, not management errors. Also, disabled individuals who start businesses hire more disabled people than do now-disabled business owners. We think that we're helping contribute to society by creating more jobs, buying more products, and so forth. It's a little switch from the welfare we know today.

Kris Mauren

One of the remarkable factoids that Urban neglected to tell you is that he does all those wonderful things on a budget in 1995 of just slightly over $50,000.

The next person I'd like to invite to come up here and tell us a little bit about their organization is Father Marino from Resources, Inc., of the Catholic Migration Office in Brooklyn, New York.

Rev. Ronald Marino, *Resources, Inc.*

My staff found out before I did that we had won, and when I came home from a recent trip there was a big note on my office door saying: "You Won." I had to explain to them that we didn't win, we were singled out, because there were several hundred winners as far as I know.

I am a Catholic priest. I live in Brooklyn, New York, and I work with immigrants. In those three particular definitions you can find the reason for the motivation, the spirit, the energy, and the results of everything that goes on in our agency. In highlighting the fact that I am a Catholic priest, you need to know that's what spurs me on and helps me inspire the people who work with me to move ahead.

This program which has been singled out by the Acton Institute, called Resources, is what I call a job-training program with a difference. The inspiration for this came from an encyclical that the current Pope wrote in 1982 on human work, where he talked about the meaning of work. We took a sentence out of that encyclical where he said, "The aim of work is not the work itself, but rather it is man."

The fact that I live in Brooklyn is important, because in Brooklyn there are people from 167 different countries who speak 80 different languages. Those are just people who have been clients or received the services of our agency and our other programs, so it is an immigrant reality. These are the people on whom every social ill is blamed. Some people say they are the cause of everything that's bad in America, and it's probably because people who believe that forget what their ancestors did and meant in America. In Brooklyn, out of 220 churches, 200 of them were built, physically and literally built, by the ancestors of people who come now. The understanding of how immigrants contribute to America is a lesson nobody's wishing to speak about or teach. As you have heard over and over again today, if people don't understand the past, they understand nothing. We try to teach immigrants what immigration has done and been in America and how they can contribute. The program is called Resources, hopefully to make them understand that they are one of the greatest resources we have—and also because I like listening to speeches, and everybody uses the word resources when they speak, and I like hearing that word.

What do we do? We have a job-training program. Right now it's a model program because we can duplicate it ourselves in other areas. We teach three things: commercial cleaning, computer graphic art, and culinary arts. Why? Because in New York City there are 23,000 restaurants. In every single one of those restaurants, you will find immigrants washing dishes. I have met many. Some of them are doctors who are studying to take the foreign doctors medical exam but need money in their pockets, and that's all they can get. I don't mean to exaggerate the presence of the medical staff in the kitchen, but there are obviously immigrants working in every restaurant, in every hotel, etc. Our cooking school is not designed to create the big chef, the famous one, although one may come from there, but simply to move the immigrant from the dishwasher to the stove.

We receive no funds from the government, and I want you to know we receive no funds from the Church, because I don't want that. I don't want the Church, the diocese, to become another government that can cut me budgetarily. They can send me to Africa, but they won't touch my budget if they didn't give me the money themselves. I decided and asked the bishop if we could just do it, just try.

Actually the culinary arts program is funded by restaurateurs, from each of whom I ask a $1,000 scholarship to sponsor an immigrant to learn. For a restaurant to give a $1,000 donation to a non-profit organization is not a difficult task. The students get the scholarships. In all our programs, the immigrants themselves have to pay something. We tell them they have to pay something, whatever that is, because someone else has paid for them, and I want them to pay for someone else after them. That's the twist that we put on the fees that we charge them, but they're obviously low. They are trained by very professional chefs, in fact, friends of mine with whom I went to cooking school. As you can see, I have a degree. I did it as a hobby and made loads of friends among chefs. Now they come and teach—some of the best chefs in New York, and some who are teachers at the Culinary Institute of America where people go, get government loans, pay that school $10,000 a year—and the same professors are teaching my immigrants in my kitchen in my center. A wonderful program.

The cleaning program—if I could have one extra minute because this explains the whole program. Immigrants can clean. We have plenty of offices and office buildings to clean, and church buildings, I might add. We have Catholic school buildings that we clean. We train them. Everyone, to get into the Resources program, must pass an English test that I designed that no one can pass, especially Irish immigrants.

We try to underline the fact that in the United States if you're serious about living here, working here, and having a dignified life, you must learn how to speak English. Before you get near the job, you have to go through English. We happen to have also 30 English schools where we can easily place them immediately, including an intensive one in our center. All the programs are taught in English. After they finish and pass the English test, which becomes very easy after I see that they have begun to go to the classes, then they learn cleaning, how to use all those machines to buff floors and wax floors and carpet washing machines and all that.

They train for a month and they train in a team. What is the team? A Chinese, a Haitian, a Polish, an Italian. They train together, the first time and the only time in New York City you'll ever see immigrants of different nationalities doing anything together, much less looking at each other in the face. One of the lessons we want to teach is just that: this unity, this ability to communicate in an international manner is the future of America, I think. I insist on that. They train for a month, and after the month is over they graduate, and they get uniforms. The uniform is blue pants and a blue shirt. It says "Resources," and it has their names. I wear a uniform every day. It doesn't bother me, but it bothers some people. You should see them when they get their uniforms and run into the bathroom and change and come out proud. That uniform guarantees me that they have clean clothes to go to work with every day and that when they go to work they're going to be clean. The people that give us work for them to do don't have to complain about sloppy workers.

They go to work—and here's where our difference is. In our company, we established three companies. We took the risk because I had done the research on job training programs in New York and found many scams. I myself tried to get into one and all they wanted me to do was take a student loan sponsored by the government. Take a loan! Take a loan! Take a loan! I don't want to. I don't want any of this. I realized that to send immigrants out into New York City to try to find jobs, even if they've been trained, is unrealistic. I knew we had to set up the companies that will hire them. We did.

We have Resources Professional Cleaning, one of our companies. We have Resources Graphic Design and Resources Culinary Arts, which in the spring will be a catering company for our cooking students to work in when they finish. The cleaning people then leave the training with their little blue uniforms and they go to places to work where we have gone out to find work. We go and say, "Let my company clean your building." We make the contract with them, and the students become our employees. They go to work. We pay them just like any cleaning company. They work six months that way.

After that, the teams are invited back to school to learn, to train to be supervisors, and they go through a month of training. The supervisors are obviously the ones that go around and check on the cleaners, liberating four or five other workplaces for the new class, etc., while they're training. At the end of that, they get new uniforms, white shirts with their names. Even better. Very few have the white shirt. Then they can go out and be supervisors.

After six months, they come back and learn how to be managers. The manager is the one who makes the proposal, goes and does the square foot measurements, the one who orders the supplies, checks the machinery, the van, whatever else there is and the manager actually learns the administrative end of the business. When they finish management training, they get ties. So, white shirt, blue pants and a tie.

Even though we're only two and a half years old, we're almost at the point where we can tell that team who are now all managers: "Listen, you guys and women, you came here with nothing, you couldn't speak English, you didn't have any money in your pocket, you never knew how to do this graphic arts or cleaning or cooking. Now you know how to run a company from A to Z. Go start your own business together. In order to help you, here are two of our contracts. Start with these. Become our competition."

We take nothing away. No American has ever come to me to ask to be in my cleaning company. They don't want to do that. We're not hurting anyone. There's plenty of work out there. There's plenty of dirt in New York. We have a big sign, "Give us your dirt." It's a wonderful experience. This thing is duplicable in other areas, too. Basically, that's what the Resources program is.

We have a whole larger immigration agency, the Catholic Migration Office of the diocese, funded by the diocese and by immigrant contributions themselves and private individuals, where we have a law firm and all those other things. Resources is something new and Resources is a rich blessing. During the course of the Resources program, people see the sign all over the place that says the aim of work is not the work itself, but rather it is man. I have a class that I teach myself, which for the sake of being modern we call Personal Development, which is a course in which they understand just what is happening to them in this program. They understand what America is all about. What immigration has meant. How to live. How to be.

We have no dropouts. We have employed 68 people already in full-time jobs. We have taken nothing away from anyone else. These people live in dignity, speak English, contribute, obey every law, pay every tax they have to pay, and are proud. Soon they will have plenty of businesses to compete with me, but they will have learned it all from us. By the way, they are hardly all Catholic. We get Muslims, Jewish people, all kinds of religions. We don't ask people their religion anyway. I tell them it's more important that we be Catholic than you be Catholic. That's it. Thank you very much.

Kris Mauren

Finally, I'd like you to help welcome Don Michele who's the CEO of the LifeChange program at the Union Gospel Mission, Portland, Oregon.

Don Michele, *LifeChange*

LifeChange is a program of the Union Gospel Mission in Portland. I run a skid-row rescue mission in Portland, Oregon. We serve some hundred thousand meals a year, but within the operation of Union Gospel Mission, we have a redemptive program called LifeChange which addresses three basic areas: crime, drug addiction, and homelessness. LifeChange is for convicted felons and drug addicts primarily, which includes those infected with the HIV virus and the homeless. We work with those deemed unredeemable by society and believe that God has a purpose for every individual.

LifeChange is a job-training program. Each resident in the community works a full eight-hour day, men and women. They work in our own business and produce 70 percent of our own income. The remaining dollars that we acquire are acquired through private grants and foundations. It's an education program. One of the guys in our program said to me: "My brother went to Penn State, and I went to the state pen." It's an education program, and each resident is required to attend our own education department, which is staffed by volunteers, and achieve a minimum of GED standard. Some residents go on to college, which we pay for, and then they work part-time within the LifeChange community and our own business after college hours.

One of our formerly homeless, drug-convicted felons has just received a 3.8 grade point average in his first quarter of college studies in electrical engineering. Now this is a 24-year-old kid who lived out on the street in front of the front door. I wish I could introduce you today to Ellen, who was a prostitute living on the corner across the street from the mission, who's now the manager of the local Subway sandwich shop in Portland. She's just a wonderful gal, 38 years old, has her whole life ahead of her, has been redeemed by Jesus Christ and learned to work in the LifeChange community, learned to work with others, and just does an incredible job. Lori Snyder is the Assistant Executive Director at Union Gospel Mission and sits on the board as an advisory member. Lori walked in the door three years ago, said she smoked $1,500 worth of crack cocaine, and was a prostitute up on one of the main thoroughfares. She has been in Life-Change for three years, done every job from cleaning restrooms to running our business, and is now the assistant executive director and hopes to start her own LifeChange community.

A lot of people ask me how we can have success without professional staff in every program area, and it's my opinion that most social services like government have too many paid professional staff. It's for that very reason—that we have limited staff—that we are successful. We have to rely on each other to make it. Nobody, but nobody, is a spectator in our community.

LifeChange is a community. We believe in overcoming together. We believe if we make it look like a duck, make it walk like a duck, make it think like a duck, eventually it will become a duck. In other words, if we make a person look successful, think successfully, act and behave successfully, he or she will become successful. LifeChange believes that everybody can teach somebody. Everybody has something to offer. Each of us in our own community has something he or she can offer to somebody else. We have a philosophy called "each one teach one." We must all rise, or perhaps stumble, together. LifeChange is a group of former addicts and convicts who have been non-producers in society, who are now a community of believers renewing the mind and rebuilding the character. Residents who've been takers from society are transformed over two or three years into givers to society. Rather than being a burden on the tax base, they become part of the tax base.

Jesus was once asked by a student of the law, "Who is my neighbor?" In his response he told the story of a man who was beaten by thieves and robbers and left for dead. We have all those people whom Jesus described in our LifeChange community. We have the thief and the robber and the man who was left for dead. Many robbed of their dignity, their possessions and nearly their lives by drugs and crime. LifeChange is simply the principles of the Good Samaritan at work in the inner cities of America. Just last month, we started a LifeChange center in Honolulu, Hawaii, just in time for winter. We've got a guy over there who has a building, has a board, and is now building a budget and we will replicate the program all over the United States, we hope. Again, my thanks and deepest gratitude to all those involved.

Father Sirico

You might also want to talk with Don later on and ask him his personal testimony and the conversion he's undergone that makes possible this program that's an outgrowth of his own conversion.

I know tonight I'm going to have to cheer up Kris because Kris manages the Acton Institute, the office, and especially the budgets, and I just have a feeling tonight he's going to be very depressed having given away $30,000, so I'll have to pray. But it is the spirit of the season!

Kris Mauren

I wanted to once again thank people who made this year possible, who enabled us to help highlight this kind of activity around the country, and I also wanted to take this opportunity to announce that we will be doing this Samaritan Award program again next year in 1996, and I ask and invite you all to be thinking of Good Samaritans in your community and nominating them.

Introduction

Jennifer E. Marshall

Our next speaker is Dr. John M. Perkins, a long time champion of Biblical justice and economic development of the black community. He founded Mendenhall Ministries in Mendenhall, Mississippi, and with others has established the Christian Community Development Association, Voice of Calvary Ministries in Jackson, Mississippi, and most recently the Harambee Christian Family Center, an after-school mentoring program in northwest Pasadena. He is the founder and publisher of *Urban Family* magazine and the author of several books, including *Beyond Charity.*

Dr. Perkins, it means a great deal to me personally to have you here today. Several years ago a friend brought me a cassette tape with a message from a remarkable lady named Colleen Evans, and it was a basic message about three "Rs": relocation, reconciliation, and redistribution. That tape really sowed the seeds of my interest in welfare replacement. I listened to it again recently and heard what I never heard before, which is the name of the person who inspired her to get the message—and the man, of course, was Dr. Perkins. His influence reaches across the nation, and the name meant something to me this time because I have discovered in the course of my work at FRC so many people who trace their inspiration back to him directly. He's raised up an entire generation of new leadership and he's transformed lives and he's done it one person at a time.

COMMITTED INDIVIDUALS

Dr. John M. Perkins, *author,* ***Beyond Charity,***
publisher, ***Urban Family,***
co-founder, Christian Community Development Association

I brought along with me Wayne Gordon, because Wayne Gordon and I today are going across America in something that we are calling the American Cities Campaign. We are taking the concepts of neighborhood and community development that have come through the church into different cities of this country. I'm the chairman of the Christian Community Development Association. Wayne Gordon is the president, and he has spent 20 years in Chicago developing ministries there. His great ministry has been raising up from that Lundale Community—one of the 15 poorest neighborhoods in America—young, indigenous people, predominantly black, who are going off to college and universities and coming back to their community and taking over the leadership in their community. He's talked about that in a book that we are carrying with us. It's called *Real Hope in Chicago.* Since I'm not going to have much time to talk to you, I thought I would introduce you to a few books that we've brought along.

The book that I think holds the philosophy that I will share with you at little bit about today is *Beyond Charity.* This book sort of outlines how we have been working for the last 35 years in neighborhood and community development. Of course, the text book today for community development is just out, and it's called *Restoring At-Risk Communities.* I edited this book, but it's written by practitioners, people who are a part of our Christian Community Development Association.

Our association is made up out of about 4,000 individuals and about 400 organizations. The purpose of that association is really not something from the top down; it's something from the bottom up. It belongs to the people. One of the things that motivated me to come here today is that I don't really believe that major organizations, whether they're government organizations or national organizations—and I've spent a lot of time working with two major national organizations on a board and I'm very discouraged with them—can implement the kind of indigenous leadership and can produce the kind of motivation and incentive that people need at the bottom.

We really need organizations that affirm the dignity of the people and inspire those people to take responsibility for their own lives. Then we can come along beside them to help them carry out their hopes and goals and aspirations.

I think you've heard today that our big federal government today is taking that incentive away. I think that's what's motivating the movement for welfare reform. You can't separate crime and violence and all these other things about people's dignity being destroyed from the fact that well-intentioned people are doing things for people and not believing in the inherent dignity of those people themselves.

The programs that I work with in our society are ones where the initiative starts first with the people themselves. Alcoholics Anonymous is working; the Steps are working, because the people in them say, "The problem is mine." Then they take responsibility, and then people come along beside them and help those people. Our work should be to bring about that kind of motivation, incentive, and creativity, and the hope in those people that they can do for themselves that which they need to do. This book talks about that.

My last book that I brought along here today is *Resurrecting Hope.* We've looked at 12 churches in America that have taken the principles that I'm talking about and have put them to work at the grassroots level in community. There's a West Los Angeles church, the largest black worshipping congregation in the United States, and they're in here. Then there's Redeemer Presbyterian Church in New York City that is in there, and there are ten other congregations that are doing that.

You'll find some copies of *Urban Family* Magazine. We created this magazine because we were concerned that the philosophy that the liberal establishment—and I'm saying that not to pit liberals against conservatives here today—has made us basically as black people think of ourselves as victims in society and that we could not do much for ourselves. People like Booker T. Washington and others came out of slavery and developed the great institutions of our day, and then here we are now with all the resources we have, but, because the government has come in and taken the responsibility away from people, we now act as victims. We fault racism and everything else for all our problems, and we never come from our advantages. And so we created a magazine we call *Urban Family* that looks at the initiatives and the people in the community that are doing things very creatively and it encourages blacks to begin to build on our strength instead of just building on our weakness and acting as victims in society. There is no other national Christian magazine that is written from a black perspective in America. The very voice and aspiration of black folks themselves are not out there outside a sort of liberal-victimization mentality that is being spoken for us by somebody else in society. This magazine is published from the urban community by people within the urban community.

The last magazine that I want to talk to you about is our latest magazine, which we've just started, called *Reconciliation*. This is our reconciler. The theories that we're operating on—even as we talk today about the church taking responsibility for the problem—are that the church itself has a major problem in America, that the major problem that the church has is that it has lost its central message of the gospel, that the gospel is the love of God demonstrated, and that the purpose of that gospel is to reconcile alienated humanity to a holy God and to each other across racial, social, and economic barriers. All our social action will not overcome that loss of the message, that apostate view, that heresy. The church is basically operating as a black church and as a white church and as a Chinese church, which is a major heresy because the very idea of the gospel was to reconcile those people together into one body and the world would know that we were Christians because of our love one for another.

Even if we take all the money from the federal government and somehow or other shift it to the local church on a basic level, it would not solve those problems because they would not be able to communicate the central message of the gospel. [Note: The Gospel, or Good News, is that Jesus Christ, by His death, offers redemption to us sinners so that through faith in Him we can be reconciled to a holy and just God by His grace.]

Let me just share with you a little bit about the philosophy on which our ministry is based. Our ministry is based on the fact that, as I heard Father Sirico talk about this morning, we are created in the very image of God. We need to reflect that image. People have dignity in society. If we confirm the dignity of people, then we can create the motivation and incentive for their own development in society.

How do you do that? How do you meet people then? The way to do that is to meet people at their basic needs as they perceive them. That's why uniform government programs organized in Washington by task forces and imposed on people down in the base level are going to further cripple people: because they don't represent their greatest aspirations. We need to start with the deepest felt needs of people. We need to love those people around those needs as they perceive them before we try to change them. We need to believe that our loving them ought to be the change agent, instead of trying to change them before we love them.

If we confirm people's dignity, if we can meet them around their deepest felt needs, then we can motivate them. That's why Jesus became bread to people who were hungry. That's why He became water to people who were thirsty. He met people at their basic needs, and He loved them around those needs, and you can't do that from afar in society.

The felt-need concept is the basic philosophy from which we look at community development. Meet people at their deepest needs, loving them around their needs and as much as possible, not necessarily accepting their behavior, but accepting it as being a need at the time, and then loving them until we can motivate them themselves to see that they've got a deeper need than that, and then begin that change in their lives.

How do you implement that then? Let's look at the three basic human needs that people have in society. The most basic need that people have in society is the need to be loved and nurtured. We know that by observing broken families that are lacking love and nurture. If you ask most urban criminologists, they will tell you that the vast majority of juvenile delinquents comes from homes without fathers, without that early childhood nurture. The greatest human need that people have is to be loved.

The second need that people have is significance, to know that they're significant. Human beings are not niggers or honkies or gooks. Human beings were created in the image of God and have absolute dignity. That dignity needs to be expressed in their own creativity. Their own creativity is work. Work, then, is absolutely crucial to the reflection of God's image. God worked, and He created us to express His dignity by creativity and by work. People need that, and we need to know how to express that.

The last need is the need for a reasonable amount of security. Everybody has that basic need. Let me say this: The most crucial problem in our society is not altogether the breakdown of the family, although that reflects the problem. The great problem we have in our society is the breakdown of the community itself. Families break down from time to time. But when the community breaks down, then the society is in pieces. Most social or government action doesn't really get at the crux of the problem. Mostly it's dealing with symptoms of the problem. In reality, it takes the village to raise the child, and so we need to re-fix the village. Mankind was created to live in a neighborhood, live in a village, live together.

When I got to Mississippi, I realized that our educational and governmental systems did not do the kind of affirming of dignity that I'm talking about, because education was to get young folks out of the village and to send them away, and the community was getting poorer and poorer. The greatest problem we have today is that people with the skills remove themselves from the places of need, and, in their stead, we send in our welfare system to make the needy dependent. What people need is our presence in the neighborhood with them. They need our inspiration.

I can see that in Mendenhall. I remember I said to my wife, Vera Mae, 30 years ago, "We're going to make a difference in this little village of Mendenhall, this little poverty village. What we've got to do is stay in this little village long enough that we can win some of those young people to Jesus Christ. We have to be able to nurture them in their faith. We have to help them get a love for God, a love for themselves, and a love for the community. That's a greater love than consumerism and materialism. Then we will help them go off to college and get education with a purpose—to bring knowledge back to the community and develop the resources of this neighborhood and community."

I stayed in that community 12 years. It happened. I left there and went to Jackson, and I stayed in that community for ten years. It happened there. Then I went to California and stayed in a neighborhood there for 13 years, and my own children there have developed a school in that community to carry on and to educate those children within that neighborhood there. It's possible to have an indigenous concept of development. The first thing is that we must go in there. The reason why Wayne Gordon has succeeded in Chicago is that 20 years ago he moved into that neighborhood and he lived in that community and inspired people.

The first "R" in community development is relocation and living in the community with the people. Outside people must come in if necessary, but the main thing is to live among the people and then inspire the people to take responsibility for their own lives. Then they can get the joy of developing their own neighborhood in their own community. Of course, it will take a generation in order for people to do that. You've got to live in the neighborhood. You can do some hopeful, nice things, but unless you are living in the neighborhood you might be convincing the poor that they don't have worth, and you might be creating more violence within those people, and you might be giving them false hopes if you don't live in that neighborhood.

The second "R" of development is that we've got to believe in reconciliation. If the church doesn't believe in that, our country will be further divided, because [the Nation of] Islam is on the increase and the new leader in the black community now is a Black Muslim.

The third "R" of development I call redistribution. Redistribution, of course, is not taking all the money from the rich and giving it to the poor, because that only means that we have deified money. That's the basic problem in our society. That's the government problem. The first need that people have—before they get money—is incentive. They need motivation. They need education. They need skills. Those are more important than money.

The fearful thing about this whole talk of government reform is that churches become contractors for the government—social agents. This is going to be a disaster for this country. I think the churches can do a lot of things well. I think the church can inspire economic and other kinds of development at the base level. But if you have churches competing for government money—and every day in the newspapers there is another church that, like government poverty programs, has misused the money—we're going to take away the last life we have within the urban community and the last healing program we have.

As you've heard today, those programs that are really healing the community are not those that are funded by the government. Those programs that are really healing the community are those where people have taken the initiative and have been able to put together the private resources to do the kind of work that we have in the community.

I would be in favor of programs like vouchers for schools and other services. At least the vouchers would be more based on production and creative competition—unlike block grants, where the resources would be wasted and swallowed up. The public schools are too big and the classrooms too clumsy to give enough nurture, and you can't bring any Christian values there.

In our community we must have the motivating force of faith. Faith-based discussions build on the dignity and the historical behavior of black people in our society. The discussion of faith must take place—or else we are destined still to be driven by racism and bigotry—and our people will still suffer.

Introduction

Jennifer E. Marshall

Dr. Virgil Gulker is the founder and president of Kids Hope USA, a new volunteer service model that places person-to-person involvement at the heart of a community's support for children and families. He is also founder of LOVE INC, an international network of over 300,000 church volunteers which has engaged church members around the world in service to their communities. He is the author of several books including *Help Is Just Around The Corner* and *Helping You Is Helping Me,* and he's also been featured in several publications such as *Policy Review* and *World* Magazine. Dr. Gulker's work answers one of the central questions that's before us: "How can you possibly even imagine a strategy that would build up a critical mass of voluntary arrangements? And specifically, how can you prepare the churches?" Dr. Gulker's answer is that you have to focus on individuals, not just the individuals in need but also the individuals who are potential volunteers. He rejects the notion that the welfare state has popularized: that you have to have some sort of special degree. In Dr. Gulker's lexicon, you don't even have to be a superhero committing full-time, just an ordinary individual with a heart to help, although he does argue that some minimal training is a help too. Here with the details is Dr. Gulker.

BRIDGE ORGANIZATIONS

Dr. Virgil Gulker, Director, Kids Hope USA

I want to thank Jennifer E. Marshall and the Family Research Council for convening this very singular gathering. I know of no other similar gathering that I've heard of or attended around the country. I think they are giving us an opportunity to discuss the critical issues facing all our communities, the church, and especially the poor.

Because it's late, because I'm from Michigan, and because I'm in Washington, there's a joke I absolutely have to tell. Recently one of your non-essential bureaucrats who was temporarily unemployed was wandering in the fields of Michigan. He came upon a shepherd. He turned to the shepherd, and he said, "If I can tell you how many sheep you have, will you give me one?"

The shepherd looked at the bureaucrat and thought, "This guy with his wing-tips and his suit and his tie, what could he possibly know about sheep?" So he said, "Go ahead."

The bureaucrat said, "You have 187 sheep."

The shepherd said, "I can't believe it! You guessed it right to the sheep!"

The bureaucrat said, "I told you I could." He stooped down; he picked up one of the animals, put it around his neck, and began to walk away.

The shepherd said, "Wait a minute! If I can tell you what you do for a living will you give me the animal back?"

The bureaucrat looked at the shepherd and thought, "I bet this guy doesn't even know what a bureaucrat is." "Go ahead," he said, "give it your best shot."

The shepherd says, "You're a bureaucrat."

The bureaucrat said, "Unbelievable! How did you know that?"

The shepherd said, "I'll tell you in just a minute, but put my dog down first."

My wife overheard someone recently calling me an expert on the care and nurture of children. She was quite amused by that comment. She simply smiled and walked away, and we haven't talked about it since. My wife remembers those times when we have done anything *but* illustrate expertise in parenting. I recall the time, for example, when I disciplined my four-year-old, and, following the discipline, I realized I had made a mistake. I had disciplined her for something that I had misinterpreted. I got on my knees and I put my hands on her little shoulders, and I said, "Emily, Daddy was wrong. Will you forgive Daddy?"

Emily looked me in the eye and said, "Sure, Daddy. I forgive you lots." I think all of you can relate to that at some level.

I have two passions. One is children and the other is the church, the body of Christ. I've listened today. I've heard about so many church-based organizations. I haven't heard much about the church. My passion is the church. I look at the 350,000 religious congregations in this country, average membership roughly 100 people per congregation, and I think of what those 35 million Christians could accomplish. The potential is awesome. We have five times more churches than post offices, yet our mail is delivered, generally. We have 35 times more churches than McDonald's restaurants. The church is clearly the most sustainable local organization, yet I hear so little about the role the church and its members can play in this process of reaching, reconciling and healing lives.

The experience of LOVE INC, says very clearly that there are Christians in every community who are prepared to help, to give hope, to share love if they are approached, if they have the appropriate training, and if they are affirmed for that relationship. As Jennifer said, what I learned with LOVE INC, through the 300,000 volunteers, was that we don't need heroes. We need very simple, very basic people. People like me and like many of you who are prepared to come alongside someone who needs principally love, nurture and affirmation.

I was challenged two years ago by an organization called International Aid to put my passions to work. They said, "Virg, can you create a model that will somehow engage church members themselves in the lives of the most at-risk children and families?" I spent a year researching that. Instead of promoting answers, I asked questions. I went to people who were involved with health services and human services, education, religion, government services, professional volunteer services. I asked them three questions. I believed at the time they were critical questions. The answers to those questions absolutely transformed my approach to ministry.

The first question: What are the needs faced by our children and families? We all read these things in the newspaper, but what do the experts say the needs are? What I heard absolutely broke my heart. If you can look at these needs, if you can look into some of the faces of these children experiencing the pain and despair that is a part of their lives, without crying, you have a problem. My heart was broken by these needs. I came to the conclusion that America either does not care for its children or it does not know how to care. How else can you explain the fact that more children in this country will be pregnant, murdered, drug-dependent, incarcerated, or poor than the children of any other industrialized country? How else can you explain the fact that children, from birth to three-years-old, are now some of the most neglected children in the entire world? One out of every four of our children lives in poverty. Thirty-one percent live in fatherless homes. The litany of woe goes on and on. I wanted to find out why there is so much need.

I went into my own community and I discovered to my dismay that in Holland, Michigan, an idyllic community along the Lake Michigan shoreline, with literally a church on every corner and an unemployment rate of 3 percent, we have a youth violence increase over the last five years of 400 percent. Four hundred percent! That exceeds the national average by 300 percent. "Why?" I asked. Why are so many of these young people getting engaged in personally and socially destructive behaviors?

Every expert said to me that it's because these young people and children are desperate for affirmation and for value. Someone needs to say to them, "You have value; you have purpose; your life has meaning in this community."

Children are looking in all the wrong places for affirmation. As John Perkins said, affirmation is the key need for all of us. We will find it. If not in appropriate ways, we will find it in inappropriate ways. More and more young people are turning toward gangs. Michigan has 83 counties. We have organized gang activity now in 44 of the 83 counties.

A 15-year-old boy in my community joined one of four major gangs, two of which came out of Los Angeles. The ceremony was as brief as it was brutal. They said to him, "Armando, all you have to do is stand here and take our beating for two minutes. Do not resist." All the men wore steel-toed boots. For two minutes they brutalized this kid. Absolutely brutalized him. At the end of two minutes, he was required to stand up, embrace each man, and call him brother. Then he was allowed, as a reward, to participate in sex in front of all the men with a girl who had also become part of the gang. The initiation ceremony for girls is, as some of you know, much, much worse.

The next day someone went to him and said, "Armando, why? Why would you allow yourself to go through that?"

His answer was immediate. He said, "I knew this was gonna hurt real bad, but I felt if I could take it for just a couple of minutes, I'd be surrounded by people who loved me." That's the name of the game, friends.

My second-grade daughter, two years ago, was asked to join a gang by a little girl whose principle characteristic was her body odor. She would crawl under the teacher's desk periodically and moan, "No one loves me. No one loves me. No one loves me." Children would not stand in line with her. They would point at her and laugh. Finally, she began to move also toward gang activity. Second grade! She wanted my daughter to go along!

My daughter did a revolutionary thing. Instead of reporting her to the teacher, my daughter began to pray for her and said to me, "Daddy, I'm going to be her friend." My daughter became her friend.

Other young people are turning to pregnancy. Talk to anyone working with pregnant girls. Ask them why these girls are pregnant. Sex has nothing to do with it. These girls in most cases are so desperate for someone to love and value them, for someone to hold them, for someone to be intimate for 20 minutes, that they will endure anything, including pregnancy. It's a desperate situation out there.

Others who do not find affirmation turn to suicide. Our suicide rate for young people is up three times—a three-fold increase in ten years. One of the second-graders whom we had hoped to work with through Kids Hope by forming a relationship is no longer eligible for our program. He tried to kill himself and was institutionalized. I was horrified. I went to the school, and I said, "You're going to have to help me with this. I have a second-grade daughter. How does a second grader come to try and kill himself?"

The teacher said, very simply, "These children, whose lives are so desperate, whose lives have no hope, conclude that death is safer than life, and they choose death." It's happening more and more.

Experts told me that we can expect to lose a generation of children. This will be the first time this has happened without a war in this country.

My next question was: "What should the church do? Do you see a role for the church?" Almost to a person they gave me the same answer. "Virg," they said, "it's really not very complex. Tell the church to mobilize its members to form one-to-one relationships with the youngest children. Tell them to go into the elementary schools and work with children who are at that critical age when values are formed, self-esteem is developed, and critical academic and problem-solving skills must be acquired. Virg, tell them to do that."

The mayor of my city, when asked what we should do about the violence in our city, said, "We don't need any more programs." Michigan, as you may know, has 40,000 non-profit organizations, not counting churches. We don't need any more programs; what we need are more caring adults to put their arms around troubled children and say, "I love you. I love you. Judy, Tom, Mary, Sammy, Armando, I love you."

Ron Vogel, former national director of the welfare program known as WIC (Women, Infants and Children), met with me once to talk about church involvement. I said, "What do you think, Ron, can a church play a role in meeting the needs of the WIC mothers and their children?"

He said, "Tell you what. I can give the churches a strategy that they can use to single-handedly reduce the incidence of infant mortality, low birth weight and long-term dependence on the public health system."

I said, "Ron, let's do it. How much is it gonna cost?"

He said, "Nothing. All I want the church to do is mobilize its mothers and its grandmothers to form one-to-one relationships with pregnant young women, talk to the young women about breast feeding, and get them to the clinic on time. If they do only that, they will transform a generation of young, black women."

Anacostia, which is somewhere around here, at that point had the highest infant mortality rate in the country. At precisely the same time I heard that statistic, an African-American young woman who worked in a ministry locally came to me and said, "We don't know what to do. We have African-American grandmothers who are complaining to their pastors and others that they no longer have any value in their church or their community." It's about people. We've got to reestablish the people issue. It's not about welfare reform. That can be a very nice intellectual dodge, but the reality is that we're talking about people with resources and people in pain.

Sometimes people who are very cynical say to me, "Virg, do you really think God is in our world?"

I say, "Absolutely. I can take you right to where he is."

"Well where would I go?" they say. I say, "At the intersection of a caring Christian and a child or other person in need. That's where my God lives. He's out there right now."

These people who won awards for their ministries, they encounter God countless times every day and every month and every year. That's the potential. Someone who works with troubled children in my area was asked recently what kinds of kids he wanted Kids Hope to work with. With what kinds of kids should we form these relationships? I expected a wonderfully learned and long-winded answer. He surprised me. He said, "Virg, focus on the children who need hugs." I've been thinking about that now for about six months. I like what that says about the potential of the body of Christ. What if the local body of Christ was known as that distinctive organization within the community that formed relationships with kids and families and hugged them? Hugged them!

I asked these people one last question: Will the church do that? They were really revved up about what could be, and I said, "Will the church do that?"

Without any hesitation, almost everyone said the same thing, "No way. We know we can count on the church for commodities, for holiday food baskets, for food pantries, for clothing closets, for rides to the doctors, for Vacation Bible School, and all that's wonderful and necessary in many cases. But we have found, to our dismay, that we cannot rely upon the church for relationships. We've had to turn elsewhere for those from other organizations."

I didn't want to believe it. I've worked with church volunteer programs for 20 years. I went out and began to survey and interview pastors, determined to prove these people wrong, because, I believe, relationships are at the heart of our gospel. John was talking about reconciliation. Without relationships, there is no reconciliation. I'm not even sure there's redemption. I surveyed pastors from churches ranging in size from 50 members to 6,000 members. I asked one question: How many of your members are engaged in one-to-one relationships with at-risk elementary school children in the neighborhood of your church? Out of a combined membership of 30,000, I found fewer than 20.

My follow-up question was: How many of your families are in relationships with some of the families? That was fewer than 10.

It doesn't make sense to me. Seventy-nine percent of all church growth is attributed to a person, a friend, or a relative telling someone about Jesus Christ, yet we're investing all kinds of money in programs and agencies. Only 10 percent of [Christian] Americans now have any significant relationships with non-believers. Ten percent. Eighty percent of all people who accept Jesus Christ do so by age 18, yet every church I went into was dedicating the vast majority of its outreach and evangelism money to programs touching people 20-years-old and up. It's a wonderful strategy to fail, and it's not reaching these kids and these families. That's the sad thing.

Do Christians care? Absolutely. I get letters and phone calls virtually every day, and I have for 20 years. When we were establishing LOVE INC, I had calls from every state. Then we began to get calls and letters from other countries. Every request sounded the same. People said, "We want to share the love of Christ with the poor, and we don't know how to do it, and our church does-n't know how to help us. Can you get something started here?"

Recently I went into a large church, and I said to them, "Your church is going into the neighborhood school in eight months to work with at-risk elementary school children. Next Sunday, I'm going to walk from this church to that school. I invite you to go with me one mile." I had a feeling that my wife, my two daughters, and I would have a very leisurely stroll. God surprised me. When I showed up at the church the next Sunday, 250 men, women and children were standing there. We walked a mile to the school and then we held hands as we circled the school. Forget church-state issues! We held hands. We prayed for those children. We prayed asking God to bless our commitment to transform and love those children.

I still have people coming up to me saying, "Virg, we needed a symbol." Mr. Woodson is here, and he said, very appropriately, that conservatives, Christians, and Republicans—not necessarily in that order—are much worse than liberals and democrats at using symbols. I'm finding that so many people want to come around this vision of helping and loving a child—especially when given a symbol.

The key problem I found in churches is not a lack of compassion. As I inquired into the organizational structure, every church I worked with had the same problem. They lacked any sort of system or infrastructure for the recruitment, training, supervision, and affirmation of volunteers. Not one had that. It's like a small business trying to operate without a personnel department. Most of these churches could characterize their ministries by saying, "We pay; we pray, and we give stuff away. We do wonderful things. Wonderful things. But we never change any lives or any situations."

Our call at Kids Hope is to go into one church at a time, to create within each individual church that infrastructure so that they can connect or engage their members in the lives of other children. My past work has all been with community agencies. I would go into communities and set up agencies drawing on the resources of hundreds of churches. I've changed. I found that, when many churches are involved in a project, every church owns it and no church owns it. The director of the church-based organization will spend 70 percent of his or her time raising money, 10 percent in managing public relations, and the rest just feeling generally frustrated.

The church is the sustainable local organization. If we can give them an infrastructure, a personnel department designed to link their members with children and families in the neighborhood, we can change the lives of the church members and the lives of the people who need help. The church simply giving out food or money or clothing is not going to make it. That's the same kind of commodity distribution that the welfare system has tried for so long, and it has not worked. We are the body of Christ. We have the most awesome potential, not just to share Christ but to share that transforming, reconciling message that can change and empower lives. That's what we can do.

We need to apply the Gideon principle. We have 35 million Christians in this country. Remember when Gideon fought the Midianites? He started with a ridiculously small army of 32,000. God stripped his army until he was left with .94 percent. If we look at .94 percent of the existing church membership, we're looking at 329,000 people (assuming the 35 million figure is accurate). If each of those people gave a dollar a week for a year, that's $17,108,000. If each volunteers an hour a week, valued at $10 per hour, that's $171,080,000. That remnant alone can contribute $188,188,000 to transforming outreach. We must not demean the potential of the body of Christ, the very means, the arms and the legs that He has given us to reach out.

Let me conclude by sharing the metaphor that has really guided my ministry. A number of years ago, during the Vietnam conflict, a number of Vietnam veterans were shipped to a hospital in San Diego. What they shared in common was that they had lost all of their arms and legs. They were lying with simply their heads and torsos on beds. They had fallen into such a profound depression that they simply could not speak. They were hiding within themselves.

The registered nurse on the floor tried everything to get them out of their depression, but she failed. Finally, in creative frustration, she called the other nurses together and said, "Gather up all of the terminally ill babies in the hospital; strap them face down to the torsos of these veterans."

As she left the room, she said to the veterans, "Gentlemen, these babies are dying. Most have no visits. No one to love them. No one to bond with. And you have nothing to do. Your job is to love these babies."

The nurses left the room. They did this day after day. In less than one week, all the Vietnam veterans had escaped their depression and were orchestrating the care of the babies. Every man fought it, but, every time he opened his eyes, the little eyes of that little baby were penetrating his soul looking for that heart of compassion that had to be in there.

Those terminally ill babies are the children and the families in our society. We're losing them. We are losing a generation of children. Those veterans are the body of Christ if it refuses to minister in the name of Christ. If it refuses to be the arms and legs of the church, the church is powerless.

We are the nurses. This meeting is so important today because it convenes the nurses. God calls us to be that creative force, to call the church, the Christian community, and the culture to an awareness not just of the need but also of what the Christian community can do in responding to that need, not simply to hold that baby up in the maternity ward just to show people how cute she is, but rather to hold the baby up and to suggest specific strategies that the church, the body of Christ, can use in reaching out to the baby, to love her, to touch her; put arms around her as she grows older, and to say, "I love you. Jesus Christ loves you. And that's going to make all the difference in your world and in my world."

One of our dear volunteers has shown the humor of God. This woman is one of the wealthiest women I've ever met. She works with Kids Hope through her church. She has been assigned to a child from one of the poorest families in her county. She noticed that Billy needed shoes, badly. The teacher said, "Don't buy them. It will cause a major disruption in the family."

The volunteer came to me and said, "Virg, it's killing me. I need to buy Billy a pair of shoes, but they won't let me." This woman could buy Billy a shoe store if she wanted to.

I said to her, "What did the teacher ask you to do? Did she ask you to buy shoes?"

She said, "No, she said, 'Minnie, could you love this boy? Could you help this boy understand how important he is?' So that's what I've been doing."

I talked to Minnie the next week, and I said, "How's that coming, that love business?"

She said, "It's incredible. I came into school last week and Billy was on the other side of the school, the other end of the hallway, and he saw me. He opened his arms and he began to run down the hallway shouting at the top of his lungs, 'Mrs. Matthews! Mrs. Matthews! Mrs. Matthews!' There he came next to me and scooped me up in a hug." This is a first-grade boy. He didn't need shoes nearly as badly as he needed love.

The church has always been there to give Billy shoes. But the Billys in our world don't need shoes anymore as badly as they need to be loved and valued. No agency, public, private, or parachurch, can do that, because their role is to respond to need. The role of the church is to respond to people. We can do it. We have the answer to this problem. We can create an army to attack these child and family problems, but we need the people, and they need the vision of a healing and loving God. Thank you.

PANEL DISCUSSION: LAUNCHING A NEW SOCIAL MOVEMENT

Introduction

Jennifer E. Marshall

Our next panel will be moderated by Don Eberly, who is the director of the Civil Society Project, an initiative seeking to strengthen civic community in America. He is the author and editor of numerous publications and several books, including *Restoring the Good Society: A New Vision for Culture and Politics.* Mr. Eberly is the founder and president of the Commonwealth Foundation, an institute promoting civic, democratic and economic renewal, and he's also the founder of the National Fatherhood Initiative, a nonpartisan civic group seeking the renewal of fatherhood in American society.

What I appreciate most about him is that he understands that the problems are much too deep for any sort of legislative fix to solve. He said recently at the Heritage Foundation: "Politicians must recognize that their ultimate success in policy reform depends precisely upon a deeper social renewal that can only originate in our hearts, homes, and local communities." The panel he will moderate includes spokesmen from both the think-tank world and the grassroots, and together they will explore what we might be able to do to form a new social revolution even while recognizing the limits of New York and Washington to address matters of the heart. Please join me in welcoming Don Eberly, who will make a few introductory comments, and then we'll hear from our panelists.

Don E. Eberly, moderator, Director, Civil Society Project

The interesting discussion this morning about libertarianism versus traditionalism centered on an idea that I think is actually very important. There are very important arguments to be made within public policy. There is also very important work to be done beyond this more sterile and fragmented debate about the actual cause and effect of the rise of the central government and what you can actually expect if the central government pulls out, and that is to promote social change by non-governmental means. It's sort of libertarian means to traditionalist or moral ends, if you will. I believe that we really do have to apply the same intellectual, moral and spiritual vigor to the business of broad-based social change that we have long applied to public policy solutions.

I asked that the panel be titled "Building A New Social Movement," or I would actually prefer "New Social Movements," plural, because I think social movements are very different from political movements. They tend to be very dynamic and grassroots and independent of political and policy affiliations.

I remember a few years ago Jonathan Rauch, who's the author of a book *Demosclerosis,* said that today's politicians and activists have turned every social argument into an argument about government, politics, or law. I really believe it's not only a question today of government over-reaching and trying to do more than it's capable of doing, but also of politics being overloaded. We have heaped too much upon politics as a place for our moral conversation and for talking about social strategies.

A lot of people are beginning to say that a lot of the action is going to have to happen outside of politics. We must ask ourselves, "What are the tools? What are the tools for promoting renewal within society, not just reform within a government?" It's largely now a settled empirical question whether social progress is linked to economic progress. Fordham University has been tracking this for 20 years, and the research indicates that, while economic progress continues to move forward in many remarkable ways, social progress appears increasingly in an inverted relationship, over a 20-year period of time. It appears like the jaws of a crocodile when you look at it. It's a 20-year trend. Economics is not the engine that's driving social progress. That's not to say that people do not need economic help and economic opportunity and that there aren't problems with joblessness and wage stagnation. There are. It's just that, as a general rule, economics is not driving social progress, nor is the state.

When Peter Drucker talked about the idea of salvation by the state being destroyed in the latter part of the 20th century, it was one of the most remarkable developments, because we used to get together and dream back in the '60s and '70s, at places like Harvard University, about how to use government as an engine for social progress. This idea that the state itself can be an engine for human progress is lost forever in our public imagination. Whether it's doing government better or doing government less, getting government in or getting government out, is an important debate, and there's a lot that's wrong with public policy, but it's just simply not enough. It may represent 10 or 20 or 30 percent of the problem.

What do you do to generate social change? Well I think for one thing, we have for too long taken too much from the social sciences, which tend to reduce man and all his mysteries and his moral nature to a hapless victim of his environment or somebody who's susceptible to help from social-service providers, and we treated man as though he was nothing but a glob of responses to incentives operating upon him, either through the market or through the state. We've got to look at social theories that are largely rooted in the sub-soil of civil society, which is faith, and re-moralize civil society.

As Gertrude Himmelfarb says, we even have a problem in civil society because a lot of private-sector institutions are not particularly wedded to Olasky principles. What would we do in today's world if we really do want to recreate a civic infrastructure in America that's based upon character and treats every individual person as though he or she is indeed made in the image and likeness of God and must be treated as a moral agent capable of moral responsibility? What would we do to rebuild a civic infrastructure?

Even as we're talking about devolution and getting government out, there's a huge discussion about the decline in social capital. By the way, I don't see social capital just as a matter of how many people volunteer and how much money we give away every year to private charity. It really goes to the actual health of our social institutions, our capacity to govern ourselves, as Michael Novak talked about it this morning, our capacity to enter into relationships and to make them work, our capacity to negotiate our way through a competitive society, to be personally effective. I think Mr. Novak's talk was very important on that point: How do we recover institutions that shape character?

I want to stress that the stakes in recovering civil society are actually a lot higher and greater than simply finding a private sector replacement for public welfare, because I think in fact the tendency to act in charity is something that's actually born of something else. It's not just a matter of our looking at civil society and saying, "Now we're going to use civil society in pure utilitarian terms to replace the welfare state." Something larger has to be happening at the level of our souls and our families and our neighborhoods. We're talking about broader social change than just acts of charity and just volunteerism. James Q. Wilson, for example, says that you can apply all the policy treatments that you wish, and it might eliminate, I think he says, only 12 percent of the problem of illegitimacy, because there is a deeper spiritual, moral and cultural problem that has to be treated. What if Wilson is right: that you can apply all the external crime controls that are available and you might reduce crime at best by 20 percent? That's an important effort to make, but as he points out, we've already mostly applied those external controls.

This emphasis on simply looking at the social pathologies of our time in the context of familiar and very convenient stereotypes is actually not very helpful because the social pathologies are increasingly moving across the social classes, and are rising actually in the case of juvenile crime and teen pregnancy at a rate faster among those who are not government-dependent than among those who are. We're really looking at models for social change that take us beyond just trying to figure out how we're going to unleash a great outpouring of concern for private charity.

Let me give you a couple of examples. As Marvin points out, in the 19th century, you had a remarkable period of outpouring of spiritual, moral, and social change that was extremely consequential at the level of community. We witnessed an explosion of voluntary associations and organizations aimed at social reform and moral uplifts and spiritual awakenings—temperance movements, private charity campaigns, children's aid societies that instilled virtue and self restraint, Sunday school movements, YMCAs, vigorous character education programs. Through voluntary means, we must recover the spirit and forms of these 19th-century movements in our time. As many of you know, I think there's a desire, an opening for many of these movements to emerge. For example, there is the "True Love Waits" campaign focusing on teen abstinence. We hear a lot about Best Friends, Elayne Bennett's program, the character education movement, the movement to recover ethics and quality in business. These movements, I think, are on the verge of major reforms in popular culture. You just get the sense that we're on the verge of major sorts of grassroots movements to reform popular culture, and especially television, and increasingly to get parents to discipline their families in the area of television.

These are all promising areas. I happen to believe for example that father absence is the most socially consequential problem of our time. The issue with father absence is not the missing paycheck. Fathers are not superfluous precisely because of what fathers do. When you have 40 percent of the children in America going to bed without the benefit of a father present and one in every two spending at least a portion of his life between the age of one and eighteen in a father-absent household, you have an enormous amount of built-in stress and social disorder that's affecting all levels of American society. How do you reverse father-absence? Is that mostly a matter of policy, or should that be done through social movements?

If we look more recently in the 20th century, we had all these powerful social movements that may or may not have involved you but they came and they affected America. The sexual revolution certainly affected how you feel about issues of sexuality; the women's movement affected how you feel, your attitudes and thoughts about gender. The civil rights movement. Environmentalism has profoundly affected how most people think about ecology, about the environment. Other initiatives and programs such as Mothers Against Drunk Driving, the Partnership for a Drug-Free America—these are quite dynamic and consequential social movements that affected attitudes, values, beliefs, practices, behaviors, etc. Most of them didn't resort to statutes to achieve social change, and this is, I think, the important point. Not that I'm against reforming statutes, but remember, as Lincoln said, he who molds public sentiment goes deeper than he who enacts statutes. He makes statutes and decisions possible or impossible to be executed.

For this panel, the suggestion was that we talk about how we might work as moral, spiritual, social, community leaders to orchestrate, direct, and summon forth a kind of change on a society-wide basis, whether for you it's in a single neighborhood or trying to develop society-wide movements. One of the big movements that I think is very promising right now is sort of a marriage movement. We've tried through the National Fatherhood Initiative to shift the argument in the direction of fathers and their unique and irreplaceable role. If you can't win the argument that fathers play a unique and irreplaceable role, we might as well all become family relativists. If you can prove that they do play a unique and irreplaceable role, then the whole superstructure of family relativism comes crashing down. At which point, then, you turn, as we must, to the subject of marriage. What is it that usually ties the father to the children? It's usually a lot of different circumstances, but usually it's a relationship to their mother via marriage. There's a place for simply promoting movements to recover marriage as a cultural ideal, and I think that may be very much on the horizon.

What do we do in today's world to recreate civic networks? To recreate moral community? It may be being born. It may be there now and of the wrong kind and need to be changed. Let me conclude with this. (I know this is not meant to be a partisan gathering and this is not a partisan point, but Michael Novak did mention it this morning.) I remember years ago, he said, the

American political party that best gives life and breath and amplitude to civil society will not only thrive in the 21st century, but it will also win popular gratitude, and it will govern. Civil society is that mediating sector of families, neighborhoods, voluntary associations, churches, charities, synagogues, the whole thing. How do we repair this vital sector of American society on which our democracy, our moral life, and our economic life as well so much depend?

Let me just run through the panelists by giving you my own personal perceptions of these very distinguished people. Bob Woodson really is the founding father of the American Neighborhood Empowerment Movement and has brought more insight to the changing concepts and techniques of how to reclaim neighborhoods, empower people, and empower families than anybody. Ronald Moore directs the program in Mississippi called Faith and Families, and we're very eager to hear about the innovative work that's being done there to throw public leadership behind the importance of churches in providing community-based charity. Terry Scanlon is with the Capital Research Center. This think tank has been doing so much creative thinking in this whole area for years, and Terry is with us and I'm eager to hear him talk about some of the key principles of discovering effective charity, what it is, what it isn't. Their newsletter has been about as effective as any publication in America in calling attention to the issue of community building and civil society and private charity and so forth. Terry, thank you for being here. Adam Meyerson is one of the leading intellectuals at the Heritage Foundation in looking at this area of citizenship and neighborhood renewal, reconfiguring his *Policy Review* journal and pointing it more in the direction of the renewal of American community. It's an exciting publication. Finally, Heather Higgins, who I would have to rank at the top of young intellectuals who are thinking through culture and community. In fact, she founded the Council on Culture & Community, and I regard her as one of the clearest thinkers and one of the most important advisors to policy makers and public leaders in the country today. If it's possible for us to hear from all these tremendous people in the time we have remaining and to take your questions, we'll try to do that, but let's start with you, Bob, and we'll move right across the table.

Robert L. Woodson, Sr., President, National Center for Neighborhood Enterprise

Since I run an organization that conducts conferences, I will take seriously the charge to be brief. The National Center aids low-income people in 38 states to achieve greater independence and self-sufficiency. We do this by going around the country and studying, not dysfunctions of low-income people, but their capacities and their strengths, and we identify them as the experts. We've learned some things out of that experience that I'll share with you, and that will constitute my remarks.

Bill Bennett at a conference not too long ago said that liberals look at low-income people as a class of victims and conservatives tend to look at low-income people as aliens. I think this is true. One of the principles that we follow, and that we find very useful, is that the goal should be not to protect people but to give them the capacity to protect themselves. Low-income neighborhoods over the past 30 years have seen $5 trillion in poverty programs parachuted into their communities by professional providers with the requirement that they participate. Now I'm witnessing conservative paratroopers strapping up, prepared to parachute in with an emphasis on what we as outsiders can do for those people inside. I think this needs to be rethought and challenged.

The other principle is that we need to strip labels from people. I think it's possible to be appalled at one group attacking another group because of their race or their religion—but without having to identify the race of the villain or the race of the victim. We ought to be against violence and insensitivity and bigotry regardless of the perpetrators.

Another point that I think would be critical is not just to offer charity to poor people but also to use the considerable political and economic strength of churches and church-goers and others to remove the kind of government barriers that prohibits faith-based organizations from properly serving their own peers. I think professional credentialing is the primary barrier that low-income providers have that is enshrined in state and local and federal policy. Certification is not synonymous with qualification. It is elitist, and those elitists are not just liberals. Poor people have to confront conservative elitism, too. If conservatives really want to make any difference in terms that empower people, they should work as we have done with Clint Bolick's Institute for Justice, *World* Magazine, and Christian broadcasting. Many of the groups that we help have transformed the lives of thousands and thousands of hard-core drug addicts by using Jesus Christ and the Gospel, yet they are confronted with state policies that require them to have master's degrees as providers. It is very difficult to get conservative politicians interested in such issues, and I think a group like this ought to look at ways that they can mobilize to remove the barriers.

The other thing we can do as a principle is to look upon some of these local providers not as objects of our charity but teachers of us because many of them have overcome some of the greatest difficulties that life ever serves up. They do not believe in rehabilitation: rehabilitation attempts to restore you to what you were before. Grassroots people do not believe in rehabilitation. They believe in transformation. They don't want the person to return to what he was before. They want him to turn into a new person, to become a new person. They are the experts at this, and there's a lot that we can learn. I would like to see scholars sit at the feet of some of these experts, question them, explore with them how they were able to do what they do, and make low-income providers the experts. It is quite possible today for people to be experts on poor people, be they left or right, and never talk to a single poor person.

The other thing that I think you can do is to stop studying failure and study success. Conservative scholars look down their noses at capacity studies of poor people. This ought to change.

Finally, I think that we need to remove the barriers that separate people across the divide. We need to disaggregate poverty.

Some people are poor because of external circumstances. For people like that, a helping hand is all they need. But the kind of poverty that troubles most of us is caused by moral and spiritual crisis, and that can be solved not by some outsider coming in offering a helping hand; rather, that outsider should strengthen local providers. What I find troubling about a lot of mentoring programs is that they assume that people and institutions that are indigenous to that community do not have the capacity to heal. I think before you rush to recruit volunteers to go into low-income neighborhoods and reach out for a child, you ought to first determine whether or not there is a local antibody that is resident in that neighborhood that is already doing that and what can you do to strengthen that local antibody to reach that child. If I were to come into your home, walk past you to tutor your children, take them to the zoo and then buy them shoes, what would it do to your relationship to your child? Let's not assume that all low-income people are irresponsible parents or that there are no indigenous institutions that could play a constructive role. I'll end on that.

Heather R. Higgins, *Executive Director,*
Council on Culture and Community

I want to talk a little bit about where we went wrong, what we aren't doing that we need to do, and why the grassroots are important. A lot of this may be stuff you already know, but some of it may be things that you don't want to think about very much just because they're the hard questions, but I think that they're questions we need to think about.

Starting with what went wrong, I think that where we went wrong in this entire debate is that we bought into this idea, somewhere between Rousseau and 30 years ago, that the perfect was possible. I ask leave to be philosophical for a minute; I do it because it underlies almost every single public policy debate we have because our underlying assumption shifted. The underlying traditional assumption about the nature of man had been that man was neither good nor bad. He was, in religious terms, fallen, but that wasn't necessarily a religious idea. It was sort of an Aristotelian idea of the view of man, and we shifted to what is known as a Rousseauean idea that man is good. If you believe that men are good, then your definition of where evil comes from has to be external social forces as opposed to a combination of external factors plus the internal decisions of individuals themselves. As a result, we got to a definition of problems as all being caused by these outside social forces, whether it was discrimination or poverty or whatever else that happened to be out there.

Along with that came the concurrent conclusion that, with sufficient will, with sufficient money, with sufficient laws, one could simply overcome these outside social forces and improve the world and create a world without poverty as the end result of our war on poverty or whatever. We forgot along the way that we are more than material beings, that we have human natures, that we have a capacity to respond to incentives, and that we are in fact in large measure agents of our own destiny no matter what those external forces happen to be. For example, as Bob just pointed out, simply because you are poor does not mean that you are a human being without dignity or without character. Several ideas followed from this, and I want to focus on three of them.

The first is that we completely corrupted the idea of compassion. Compassion classically defined is exclusively an individual virtue, not a public one. We have turned it into a public virtue that is defined by state programs to assist victims of those external social forces, something which in and of itself becomes uncompassionate because you can't do that without creating an injustice for someone else down the line. That in turn corrupted the entire language of compassion. If you think about it politically, *compassion* became a code-word for increased government funding and increased state programs. This meant that the very people who believed they personally had a greater calling to personal compassion, because they didn't believe that the state ought to be doing this, abandoned the very language of compassion. What we were left with for 30 years was a very weak and pitiful me-too-ism. If welfare worked, speaking about welfare as one example, I think that we would all be for it. The problem with welfare is that it is antithetical to the very principles of human nature as it is presently designed, and therefore cannot work.

Finally, I think, the third consequence of this and what went wrong is that we bought into a standard of moral virtue that said what mattered was the amount of will that you exerted, generally in the form of the degree of rhetoric that you were willing to employ and the amount of other people's money that you were willing to commit through taxes. That became the standard of your degree of moral virtue. Remember: Will is what matters, if suffering is purely a result of external social forces. We completely forgot the idea of looking at the outcomes that are achieved, in terms of assessing what works and what doesn't, what is worth doing and what is not, what is in fact true charity and what is not.

Following from these three things, let me give you some ideas of things that we need to do that I think we are not yet doing sufficiently (beyond demonstration projects, which are tremendously important). I personally get very annoyed at what I think is an absurd argument: that if the government doesn't spend the money, then somehow the money will evaporate. If the government doesn't spend the money, the money does not evaporate. What we are simply talking about is shifting the same amount of money and funneling it through other forms, whether it's through tax credits or whatever it might be.

I do think that there is a very important concern out there that we tend to gloss over. We must remember that most of these changes occurred because somebody was very ill-served by what went before. We have in our society—and I think we do ourselves and others a gross disservice when we gloss over this fact—people who in their own lifetimes remember state structures that were highly discriminatory, who in their own lifetimes felt compelled to march holding up signs saying, "I am a man," which is I think one of the most disturbing things that somebody could ever feel that they had to tell us in that way. To assume that everyone is going to know that we are proceeding with good will is a great mistake.

I have no patience with the questions of finance, but I understand completely the questions of intention, and I think that it is very important that we think about this and make clear how we would have sufficient and sustained good will to carry off any system that is not dominated by government programs. How would we handle a transition? How would we speak to the poster-children whom I think we can all anticipate and whom we would use if we were conducting the campaign *for* government funding of all these programs, as opposed to private or religious funding. We need to understand and address all these real concerns.

Second, alongside what we need to do, there is the important area of language. We need to relearn the language of moral argument, of genuine compassion, and of high-minded principle, something which is only now slowly coming back into the debate, but something that we all need to internalize and use. We need to be self-conscious about the words we use. So often the words we use are in fact not the words that we really mean, but they've become habits of the culture.

Let me give you two examples. The word *values* is something that the progressives dreamed up precisely so that they would not have to use either the language of virtue or the language of principle, virtue being internal, principle being external. They are not *values,* which are highly relative, ever-shifting, and cannot be weighed one against the other.

The word *government* used to be only rarely used without a modifier in front of it. There was never a notion that there was just government. Rather, there was civil government; there was self-government; there was church government; there was business government; there was family government. We need to reintroduce the idea that there are various spheres of government that have their various appropriate levels of responsibility. These are only two examples, but until we start controlling our language we will have a very hard time controlling the debate.

Finally, and most importantly, there is a tendency to focus on what is wrong and not also to remember to paint a picture of what can be right, to remember to have an affirmative vision of where we are going and why we are going there. You cannot sell something unless you have a picture of what it is that you are trying to sell. The Olasky piece today on abortion and adoption was a very good example of understanding the images that he wants to "sell" to young single mothers who are considering single parenting about the advantages of adoption both to themselves and to their children and of changing the entire framework and perception of that debate. We need to remember to use images. We tend to be highly intellectual, thinking in terms of numbers and arguments, and we tend to get frustrated if people don't understand the clear light of our argument and need anything more than that. The reality in this world is that you tend to sway people by moving their hearts, and you move hearts by using images. The types of images we should be thinking very hard about are positive, affirmative images of who can be helped, and how, by exactly the types of efforts that we're talking about.

Also, it is important to show the negative images, the ones that paint clearly the problems that are out there if one follows the prescriptions that we presently are living under. Two examples of this: the Wenatchee case, which I hope you all have been reading about in the *Wall Street Journal.* [Editor's note: The reference is to Wenatchee, Washington, where a wave of bogus child-abuse prosecutions was touched off by an over-zealous policeman and a few therapists. People are still in jail there because of accusations long since recanted.] I think that this is just immensely important to anyone who is interested in fighting the family values debate and the parental rights amendment movement. It is very important to show the victims of the excesses of the current "compassionate government" child protection system, the unintended victims, to show that there are costs to all these noble intentions.

Another example would be the homeless organization in New York that went up against Grand Central Partnership and made a point of deliberately having an in-your-face attitude and keeping homeless people out on the street, not wanting them to go into jobs programs and get assistance, because the group's objective—and some of this is on videotape—was very explicitly to have the homeless be on the street and suffering so that the rest of us could not get along in life and pretend that they didn't exist. They were not interested in helping homeless people; they were interested in advancing their own advocacy position and their view of the larger society. We need to be very conscious about bringing forward images of what doesn't work so that we can prepare the ground better for what does.

Fourth, I make this point particularly because a lot of this conference has focused on the issues of welfare, family values, parental rights—the whole nine yards. On these issues, what we have forgotten to do is to address the problem of the tyranny of blood. What do I mean by that? One of the oldest ideas in the Judeo-Christian religion, if you look back to the Old Testament in Genesis and Exodus, and indeed throughout, and then again if you look at the idea of America itself, is the idea that we moved beyond being tribes who are defined by whom we are born to, that we are no longer limited to blood relations, but we are a community of affiliation and ideas. The ideas we subscribe to are what make the difference. When you had that six-year-old girl up in New York who was molested by her mother and found dead just two weeks ago, you found that the left was saying, "See, this is what you would have if you had parental rights and family values." Quite the contrary: it is the programs of the current social service workers who do hideous things precisely because they believe that families are based on blood, not on affiliation. Of course, blood originally gets the benefit of the doubt and some primacy via legal presumptions, but as soon as the obligations of blood are abandoned, then there is a higher obligation to the child to the affiliation of the new family. I know that Conna Craig, who's here, can speak so elegantly on this from personal experience. That is a very important and defining issue that we need to articulate carefully.

Fifth, we need to conduct a campaign to explain that we are on the side of charity—but that we are not on the side of random charity—a campaign that makes very clear that there is good charity and there is bad charity. The dividing line is not necessarily whether it's government or private. There are many private charities, many private foundations that do miserable, counterproductive work, where no charity would be far better than the bad charity they offer. We need to start thinking and redefining, going back to the 1800s. We've had a huge shift in the definition of what it is that even constitutes charity, and we need to develop standards of accountability by which these charities are measured and reviewed.

All these ideas are very important to those of you who are in the grassroots. They become part of the message that you convey through the projects that you engage in. Your work is so important on two grounds, both because of the process of ideas and because of the essence of citizenship itself. Ideas move from being held by a few people to being held by the community at large. You are the last and most important step in spreading those ideas and changing the culture. Without changing the culture, you will not change the laws, you will not change the expectations of your fellow citizens, and all that is crucial to any effort to re-limit government and to return to some idea of a virtuous citizenry.

Rev. Ronald Moore, *Mississippi Faith and Families Program*
So often we're concerned about being politically correct. Since I'm a Baptist preacher, I don't have to worry about that. If I were an atheist this afternoon, I would tell you that man perhaps crawled up out of a slime pit and, in his crawl, he lost his tail, that man wasn't created, he evolved. But I'm not an atheist; I'm a Baptist preacher, so God created man. If I were a black Muslim today, I would tell you put all your faith and trust in the Honorable Elijah Mohammed. But my Bible tells me that my Savior was born in Bethlehem. Elijah Mohammed was born in Georgia. My Bible tells me that my Savior would die one Friday afternoon on a cross. Elijah Mohammed died in the hospital. My Bible tells me that my Savior would get up on the third day's morning. Elijah Mohammed's been dead a long time, and he hasn't gotten up yet. All my faith and trust is in Jesus Christ, because I believe that Jesus Christ changes lives.

A few years ago, before Kirk Fordice was elected Governor of Mississippi, many people were wondering what are we going to do about this decadent mess that we have in that state. We have the poorest state in the nation. We've got the highest rate of unemployment. We've got the highest rate of teenage pregnancy and we have more children being born out-of-wedlock than any other state in the Union. We've got some problems. Finally, our governor, after riding through our state and looking at this decadent mess that we have going from housing complex to housing complex, going from community to community, just threw up his hands and said, in effect, "Listen, government created this mess; maybe government can help fix it, but not alone. Government can help, but this problem has to be turned over to an entity that has been empowered to change not just conditions, but also, the lives of individuals. This needs to be turned over to an entity that doesn't just treat the effects of problems, but can treat the cause of the problems." He asked the local churches to become involved in the lives of welfare recipients.

We've spent, someone said earlier, over $5 trillion in this war on poverty, and in Mississippi we've had every job training program that you can imagine. We've had every food program, every program that you can imagine to help the homeless and help children that have been born out-of-wedlock, and we're still in the same condition we were in some fifteen years ago.

What needs to be done? Well, first of all, we realized that we had to get the churches involved. That we needed some positive, grassroots action from the local level to engage the lives of these AFDC families. The governor of our state asked each of our churches (we have 5,500 churches in Mississippi) to adopt at least one welfare family.

We have 55,000 AFDC recipients in Mississippi. Probably 80 percent of these families are headed by African-American mothers. They read perhaps on a sixth-, seventh-, or eighth-grade level, and most of them have four to five children, and they haven't worked in the last ten or 12 years, and they've all been on AFDC all their lives.

In Mississippi we have the only state/church family partnership right now in the nation. The program is called Faith and Family. We asked that each and every church adopt one family referred to that church by the state. Each and every family is an AFDC family. We asked the church to adopt the family, determine the needs of that family, and address those particular needs. Each and every church has some idea of how they're going to address a particular need of a particular family because those families are normally centered around that church. Normally, the church members are aware. They know these particular individuals, and the church is the only entity that can provide that one-on-one intervention.

In Mississippi, we have case-workers who work for the state. Each case-worker has about 250 clients that they simply call up and say how are you doing, and they hang up the telephone. We wanted to reverse the ratio. Why not, instead of having one case-worker to 250 welfare clients, give one church with 250 members one AFDC family? You've got 250 people seeing about one family. We've been able to change some things with that, because we have jobs programs in our state that have spent up to $400,000 and have yet to put anybody to work. We have other programs that were supposed to work with the poor or with the homeless, and we see no results of their work basically because they've been trying to work with individuals from the outside. The church is able to work with them from within. We don't want to change just the conditions; we want to change the person, because if you change the person, the person can change her own conditions.

When you walk into housing complexes, you can walk into some apartments, into one apartment and into three others without ever going outside because you have people who live there who don't care. They have no hope. They have no responsibilities. Since there's no responsibility, there's no sense of accountability. We realized that there has to be a great change. As the church adopts the family and begins the program to change the life of this family, to upgrade this particular family, to change their life from a life of dependency upon the government to a life

of self-sufficiency, they move through that with a series of courses, and each and every church has gone about doing this differ-
ently. Some of them have taught basic hygiene, grooming, and
preparing resumes. All this is taught from a biblical perspective.
In the past, in our jobs programs, they've been able to go to
school, sit there for an hour or two, hear what the teacher has to
say, and leave. They go back the next day and the next day, and
they're in the jobs program some 10 or 15 years, and they never
find jobs, because the real need hasn't been met. We've been able
to address the real need of the family.

This has really upset a lot of people because they really don't
understand the concept of what we're trying to do in Faith and
Family. No one is trying to proselytize families. We're trying to
take them and ask the church to find out what their needs are.
We introduce them to a divine entity, and hopefully they'll accept
that, but, if not, then at least we teach them other life coping
skills so that this family can leave a life of government dependence and start a life of self-sufficiency.

It is so simple. It is simply going back to the basics. We have
young ladies who are on AFDC and have never worked. One
becomes 18 or 19. She has a child; she moves out of the home of
her mother, moves into an apartment, and is asked to take care
of that apartment. She receives a welfare check of $96 a month,
a utility voucher of $86 a month. She's given a Medicaid card and
$306 of food stamps, and they say, "Listen, live your life." They
put her in an apartment and they expect her to take care of it,
but she doesn't know how to wash dishes; she doesn't know how
to comb a child's hair; she doesn't know anything about proper
grooming; she knows nothing about health and proper hygiene.
Consequently, when that child leaves home, he goes to school
and he tears up the classroom. Consequently, when she leaves
home and goes and tries to find a job, she'll go into the person's
office who's going to hire her or interview her, with five or six ear-
rings in her ear, six or seven in the other ear, an earring in her
nose with braids all in her hair because she has no concept of
what proper grooming should be like.

We're just simply going back to basics. We're teaching them how to say, "Yes, ma'am," and "No, ma'am. Yes, sir. No, sir." How to carry themselves. How to dress properly. How to spend their food stamps. Finally and hopefully, we try to get them to accept Christ or try to get them to change their total concept of the religious community. Hopefully, they will join a church, but we can't proselytize. If they decide to, that's fine. If not, we don't worry about that. With the state, the church, and the family working together, we've been able to take girls who've never worked in their lives, who've been parts of other jobs programs, who work with those programs, who haven't been able to find employment; we've been able to put each and every one of these families to work.

In the state of Mississippi now, we have about 190 churches involved in Faith and Family over this one-year period. Out of those 190 churches, we have a total of about 200 families involved. At this particular time, eight families have been moved totally off welfare; another 55 are about to come off of welfare. We have another 206 churches about to enter the program. If every church in Mississippi would adopt five families, we would have half of our AFDC population off welfare and into a work environment within a one-year period.

We are also addressing the residual effect of what has happened. We've been able to see a young lady whom we've taken into the church and trained in life coping skills and taught how to take care of herself go back home and take Clorox, take detergent, and clean up that filth that she had been living in for the last 10 or 15 years. It's remarkable how, when that change takes effect in her life, she'll go back, and, instead of passing the telephone from apartment to apartment, she'll take sheet-rock and nail it up to the wall. Take masking tape and mask it. Paint her house. She learned that she needs to be responsible, that she has to be accountable, that, if she wants to go up, she's going to have to be able to change her attitude. We've been able to do that with each and every family we've adopted.

The state's role in this program is simply to refer families to the churches and to offer their ongoing technical assistance. The case management entity stays involved, because they're the advocate for that particular family. Now one problem with our program, and you might find this in your state, is that there is a huge welfare bureaucracy in Mississippi, and they've tried everything that they could do to tear down Faith and Family, because the case-workers feel that they are going to lose their jobs and that the churches are going to become case-managers. The social workers feel the churches are going to become social work entities. A few months ago they started sending us families with sixth-, seventh- and eighth-grade educations, and everybody was saying, "Listen, there's no way that you're going to be able to place these people. They can't do anything. Most of them can't read. They can't write. They don't know how to talk. What are we going to do with them?" Our governor was a little worried about that.

Within the last month, we put together a database of about 15,000 families in Mississippi. Each of these 15,000 families has a specific need: domestic help. They need someone to wash dishes, clean floors, wash the windows, and take care of children. We're going to refer these sixth- and seventh- and eighth-grade clients. We're going to train them and refer them to those people who need domestic workers. Domestic work in Mississippi is not like it was forty years ago. Domestic workers make $250 to $350 per week. Most of them have medical and dental coverage. What I'm simply saying is that every individual can find work, and whenever they find work there is a sense of dignity. It develops dignity. It develops accountability. It develops responsibility. Their moral and their ethical lives are changed. I'm not talking about temporary change; we're talking about a permanent change.

Terrence Scanlon, President, Capital Research Center

I'm Terry Scanlon, and I'm president of the Capital Research Center, and I thought I might just give you a minute or two on the work of the Capital Research Center, because I think it will be a valuable resource to you all.

We've been around for about twelve years. We were founded by Willa Johnson, a great lady, who started on a shoestring. We call ourselves philanthropic watchdogs. That's a simple definition, and I think it's an accurate one. We produce three monthly publications. One is *Philanthropy, Culture and Society*. Marvin Olasky, by the way, was the first editor of that publication and has been a frequent writer of ours for 12 years. We seek out good charities, and we write about them. The ideas that they pioneer could be replicated in other areas.

The second publication we call *Organization Trends*. It's a hard-hitting publication. We look for charities that aren't doing what they should be doing, often not following their original donors' intents. In our current issue, we go after the Annie Casey Foundation in Baltimore, which was started by executives of the family of the founders of UPS, the parcel service people. It's a very large, multimillion-dollar foundation, and their money in our opinion is certainly going to the wrong groups. The idea is to expose that, obviously with the idea of rectifying it, and in some cases we can actually achieve that.

Our third publication is *Alternatives*. We look at different things. Conna Craig is our current author. She did a very fine piece on adoption, and I commend it to you. We hit other areas. We had Heather Richardson just recently as one of four foundation directors talking about the new political climate in Washington and what effect that would have on charities.

We do monographs. We do a directory every year, *Patterns in Corporate Philanthropy*, where we track the giving of the top 250 Forbes companies, and that list changes every year because it goes by sales. This year, we will be out in about five weeks, and we'll track the giving in the public policy arena. That is the only thing that we get involved with. We give a grade for the company's performance. Regrettably last year we gave only one A, and that was to the Eli Lilly pharmaceutical people in Indiana. We had four Fs. I commend that book to you. The grades change. Some companies, I think, do a better job as a result of the publicity. Last year, *Forbes* Magazine did a big write-up on some of the failing companies, and two of those companies came in to see us and asked what might be done to get a better grade. Discussion of a civil society was part of the presentation. It's interesting to see their reasons for change. It's not always the right ones, the altruistic ones, but better change for the wrong reason than no change at all with many of these groups.

We're doing a guide, a non-profit advocacy guide that will be published about the end of January, where we look at 500 non-profit advocacy groups. We give a grading. We describe their work and their funding sources. For the very first time, this year we'll include the portion of federal moneys that each of these groups gets. That's probably one of the hardest bits of information to get from these groups. Many non-profits don't want to tell you a) that they even solicit federal money, b) that they take it, c) how much they get, or d) what part of their total budget is federal money. For the first time, we'll have that kind of information.

Jonathan Adler is doing a very interesting piece for us, which will also be published next month, on the environmental movement, who the environmental groups are, who funds them, horror stories, success stories, and the issues that the environmentalists will probably be emphasizing at the turn of the century. It can be a very useful guide for people interested in that movement.

Tom DiLorenzo, a professor at Loyola in Baltimore, is doing a book right now on the age lobby. He's taking a serious look at the American Association of Retired Persons (AARP), the National Council of Senior Citizens, and several others, and will look at each critically, talking about the programs that they've been advocating and the federal moneys that each of these receives. It will be astounding to many people. AARP last year received about $86 or 87 million from the federal government. One of their programs is warning seniors about the hazards of the ozone layer. Hopefully, by publicizing these we'll make a more sensitive Congress aware of some of the grants that have been given to these groups. In our minds, moneys could be given to much better groups and for better purposes.

Much of what I have prepared has been mentioned today. I did want to mention one thing though about advocacy groups, because they are growing and they're becoming a bigger part of the so-called non-profit sector.

There are over a million groups now that are 501(c)(3), or, as we call them, tax-exempt charitable and advocacy groups. Last year alone, 45,000 new groups joined the IRS rolls as tax-exempt. It's important to distinguish which of these groups are true charities and which ones are advocacy groups. Regrettably, the advocacy groups are growing. Many of them masquerade as charities. One, though there are many that would fall in that category, is the Children's Defense Fund, which many of you are familiar with, headed by Marian Wright Edelman, now with a budget of several million dollars. Not a penny of that CDF money goes for a child. It's all advocacy lobbying, doing a big job now in fighting the welfare reform bill that was passed by the majority of both Democrats and Republicans in both houses of Congress.

Other charities are becoming essentially non-profit conduits of federal funds. Regrettably, Catholic Charities now gets 60-something percent of its budget from federal, state, and local moneys. We write about that. We think that's a mistake. We think the personal charity that we've been hearing about today is going by the wayside.

We're all donors here, whether big or small—I guess most of us are small—and I want to just give you a few pointers on that. I would urgently stress that you review all the past publications and the current projects of any groups that you support. Find out what portion of their budget comes from federal sources. It's regrettable that, as more charities become high-status, if you will, they really lose the original fervor—the religious fervor, if that's what they were set up for—and the morals that had been taught as part of that charity. They become very secularized, and that's a growing problem in American charities today.

Also, we should be smart about our giving. It's interesting that individuals who often start foundations are very serious about acquiring wealth but often very frivolous in giving it away. We ask ourselves every day, "Why is that the case?" Also, we should be sure that our motivation for giving is the right one. Often, people are looking for social prestige or making connections. That's a mistake. They give out of guilt. That's a mistake. Often now in giving to colleges, it's almost a nostalgic thing, which is why people give to colleges and universities that have changed drastically since they went there. Some schools change dramatically in five or six years. Don't give to your *alma mater* based on your recollection, faulty or otherwise. Go there today and look at it. Talk to professors. Talk to students. Talk to students who are part of religious groups that probably could give you a better feel for what's going on.

I'll stop there and be happy to answer any questions. I did want to commend the Family Research Council for putting this symposium together. I think it's very valuable.

Adam Meyerson, Editor, Policy Review
I'm Adam Meyerson of the Heritage Foundation. My colleagues at Heritage and I always feel we're with family when we're with the Family Research Council.

I know the hour is late. You've listened to a lot of inspiring speeches. As Henry VIII said to one of his wives, I promise not to keep you too long.

Don Eberly said some nice things about our magazine, *Policy Review: The Journal of American Citizenship*. This is a new magazine. We redesigned it at the Heritage Foundation. We will be specializing in studying success stories in the Bob Woodson mode. Success stories of organizations that are putting the family back together, that are solving crime, reducing crime, that are producing superior education for poor and working class children, that are providing opportunity, that are finding real homes for kids who need homes. There are so many success stories out there; this is the great news about America.

We are going through a period of great social entrepreneurship in this country. We've heard a little bit about this through this great program that Jennifer has put together, but the Good Samaritan Awards of the Acton Institute, the work that Virgil Gulker and John Perkins and so many others have been doing is the tip of an extraordinary iceberg of social entrepreneurship as private institutions and local governments are stepping up to the plate to solve problems where the federal government has struck out. Whether it be Promise Keepers or Best Friends or community policing or profit-making organizations that are doing a great job doing job training, we are seeing all sorts of innovative organizations solving problems. The American spirit of ingenuity is alive and well, and it's solving a lot of the terrible problems that we have in this country.

Now, when I heard so many of the inspiring presentations today, it occurred to me that this is what the winners of the Good Samaritan Award are doing, what Virgil Gulker and Ron Moore and so many of the people who have spoken today, and the people who work with Bob Woodson, are doing. They are doing what the founding fathers wanted Americans to do. This was the kind of self-governing republic that they had in mind. Some of the people that Bob Woodson works with may not have read Madison or Jefferson, but they are doing what Jefferson and Madison wanted. They may not think of themselves as conservatives, but they are practicing the conservative way of life, and the central challenge for conservatives is to support them. Find out what their obstacles are, champion them, help them, not so much through government money but by showing success stories, demonstrating what those success stories are, overcoming obstacles that come from the courts and from the federal government and state and local government (frequently state and local government is a bigger problem), and especially that awful virus of credentialism that Bob Woodson talks about.

This principle of building civil society, of going back to the principles of our founding fathers, is the central challenge for conservatives over the next twenty years, and it's interestingly the principle that brings all the conservatives together. The libertarians like this because of the emphasis on a free society, of voluntary, non-governmental institutions that solve most of our problems. The religious conservatives like it because of the emphasis on faith; it's religious organizations that are going to be solving most of the problems with the emphasis on faith and family and responsibility for the needy. The growth-and-opportunity conservatives like it because economic liberty is a central part of true citizenship. Also, the nationalists who are worried about what's happening to the American way of life or concerned about the loss of national identity and patriotism will like it because this is what the American way of life is all about. If we can restore the American way of life by focusing and strengthening local institutions, we will solve the concerns that the nationalists are talking about.

Not only is it what the different branches of the conservative movement are most concerned about, but there are also actually a lot of honest liberals and centrists who are going to be interested in this, and I think we should make a serious effort to get them to join our movement.

I will close here. I want to leave you with one wonderful quote from Helen Keller: "The world is moved not only by the mighty shoves of the heroes, but also by the aggregate of the tiny pushes of each honest worker." I hope all of us will join in this important movement to save America.

Jennifer E. Marshall

Well, Mr. Meyerson has really summed up the day quite nicely, so I just want to close by saying that I think in the end we're going to adopt our answers by default, because there's no alternative strategy. At the moment, we really sort of have two competing alternatives. Either we create an underclass and we treat them as wards of a custodial state and we just spend lavishly to keep them comfortable while we ask them to leave us alone, or we can begin restoring functions to neighborhoods and communities and churches. I think the fate of our experiment with self-government really depends on our capacity to begin renewing a sense of responsibility, but across all income brackets, coupled with a renewed commitment to our founding fathers' faith that all men are created equal to live up to those responsibilities.

APPENDIX I

THE GREATEST OF THESE IS LOVE:

A FAITH-BASED ALTERNATIVE

TO THE WELFARE STATE

In an 1844 essay titled "True and False Philanthropy," American preacher William H. McGuffey unwittingly diagnosed the ills of the modern welfare state. McGuffey draws a contrast between a "Mr. Fantom" and a "Mr. Goodman." Mr. Fantom begins: "I despise a narrow field. O for the reign of universal benevolence! I want to make all mankind good and happy."

Mr. Goodman responds, "One must begin to love somewhere; and I think it is natural to love one's own family, and to do good in one's own neighborhood, as to anybody else." Mr. Goodman laments of Mr. Fantom, "And so, between the great thing he cannot do, and the little one that he will not do, life passes, and nothing will be done."

Today, moral relativism has driven a wedge between those reformers who hope to promote moral uplift and those who aim only to relieve material needs. But in 1844, Mr. Fantom and Mr. Goodman did at least agree that the object of benevolence was "goodness" and "happiness"—or, in more sophisticated parlance, virtue and individual fulfillment. Mr. Fantom and Mr. Goodman parted ways in defining the means to achieve those ends, and their differences frame the central questions confronting contemporary reformers.

First, should the locus of our action be the individual or the collectivity? Are we intent upon "making all mankind good" by coercion, as Mr. Fantom aspired, or in "doing good" in the context of freedom, along with Mr. Goodman?

Simply limiting the size of the welfare state will not yield a sparkling rebirth in the nation's naked cities. Limiting government will be necessary, but not sufficient, to repair cultural rot. The insufficiency of libertarian means, however, does not imply the existence of some proactive political means that will be adequate to the task. Restoring our society will require embracing a vision of moral autonomy and inherent dignity for every individual.

Individual or Collectivity?

Nature has revealed two fundamental truths about man. He is perpetually weak and flawed, but also rife with potential for love and renewal. Personal failing, in fact, often contains the seeds of renewal because it discredits an exalted sense of the self. By reflecting on the dynamics of human weakness, reason itself can apprehend a higher law rooted in God, to whom man must hold himself accountable.

Conservative theorist Frank Meyer argues that the cornerstone of civic morality in the West is the Great Commandment "to love the Lord thy God with all thy heart and thy neighbor as thyself." In reflecting on this mandate, Meyer introduces a paradox. By ignoring utterly everything but God and individual persons, the world's most famous invocation to selflessness has established the individual squarely at the center of the Western tradition. The individual must be "the central moral entity, and society as but a set of relations between persons—not as an organism morally superior to persons,"[1] Meyer writes, because "no community, no state, no association—only persons, individual human beings—can receive the beatific vision or be redeemed by the divine sacrifice of love."[2] The words are radical in implication. They ask those who believe in the divine sacrifice of love to acknowledge that healing the culture will depend on the interaction of individuals, not the clash of abstract political entities.

The concept of "interaction," of course, is a necessary corollary to the emphasis on the individual. Meyer's vision of social harmony, after all, rests on a vision of the individual redeemed, and man is redeemed only by acquiring a sense of something larger than himself. Through a rich and vast array of daily interactions with each other, individuals mature into complete human beings with a sense of self-control, but also a sense of connectedness and mutual obligation. The state's role in fostering man's nobler impulses depends ultimately on nurturing, not individuals directly, but all the small groupings into which human beings organize themselves—outside of and distinct from government.

The moral superiority of individuals meeting each other face to face, in the space we call "civil society," emerges with particular force in the story of a woman named Clara Hale. A poor woman in her mid-60s, living in a poor neighborhood, Clara Hale took in a baby born with a drug addiction and went on to found Hale House, a group home for addicted children in Harlem. "It was Clara Hale who did this," Michael Joyce writes, "not an expert, not a bureaucracy. Had she exercised her citizenship in the modern, tragically devalued sense of that term, Clara Hale would merely have advocated, through voting and political activism, more programs for state-funded professionals to care for these children of God." But she did not turn away from them and speak to society, in the abstract. She held each child, one by one, and spoke their names to them. "Clara Hale's sense of citizenship, her active and direct participation in service to her fellow man, displays the vibrancy and proves the superiority of civil society,"[3] Joyce concludes.

The proliferation of need is a cry for a new generation of Clara Hale's, with an acutely personal sense of moral responsibility.

Freedom or coercion?

If the moral development of the individual is the central concern, then liberty and virtue must be the twin ordering principles of political and social life. The pursuit of virtue is the highest moral good, but it cannot be a political question. Virtue depends on individual freedom of choice and can be neither exercised by collectivities nor achieved by political coercion. F. A. Hayek once wrote:

> Freedom is the matrix required for the growth of moral values—indeed not merely one value among many but the source of all values. It is only where the individual has choice, and its inherent responsibility, that he has occasion to affirm existing values, to contribute to their further growth, and to earn moral merit.[4]

The only political means to promote virtue, then, is to establish and maintain freedom for the individual.

If virtue depends on the preservation of liberty, however, it is also true that the maintenance of liberty depends on the status of virtue. The meaning of freedom encompasses much more than the absence of coercion or an abundance of options. Because a democratic society requires citizens to be capable of governing themselves, freedom cannot be an end in itself. As Lord Acton put it, "Liberty is not the freedom to do what you wish; it is the freedom to do what you ought." Libertarian means, in short, must serve traditionalist ends, while traditionalism must resist the temptation to use coercion to promote its own ends.

The only satisfactory balance between virtue and freedom is a vibrant civil society, that sphere of life that includes all the institutions and interactions that stand between the individual and the total state. While the elemental building blocks are the family and the church, civil society also encompasses the Boy Scout troop that builds hiking trails for the community, the school that teaches young ones how to read, and the homeless shelter that keeps its doors open thanks to dedicated volunteers. Civil society may be as formal as the Red Cross chapter that has secured its 501(c)(3) tax status or as informal as an afternoon gathering of young mothers at a neighborhood park. It is both Hale House and your house. Sharing stories around the dinner table, holding hands with a new widow, or looking men directly in the eye at the local soup kitchen—this is the stuff that softens hearts and melts social barriers. By maximizing opportunities for service to one another, civil society promotes the strength of character that safeguards against freedom's atomistic tendencies.

The freedom that allows civil society to thrive is, in fact, much more likely to engender strong communities than the isolated individuals of liberal myth-making, for human nature predisposes man to live life in communal settings. Alexis de Tocqueville wrote in *Democracy in America:*

> The township is ... so well rooted in nature that wherever men assemble it forms itself. Communal society therefore exists among all peoples, whatever be their customs and laws. Man creates kingdoms and republics, but townships seem to spring directly from the hand of God.[5]

The prospects for civil society do depend critically, however, on the preservation of the nuclear family as the basic unit of society.

A Revival of Family

While his name is almost synonymous with self-interest, Adam Smith also observed a near-universal human attribute of sympathy that he identified as the source of human moral sentiments. Although distinct from altruism, Smith's notion of "sympathy" inspired man to seek the approval of his fellow citizens by functioning in ways that sustained healthy communities. Endorsing Smith's hypothesis, John Adams wrote in 1790, "As Nature intended men for society, she has endowed them with passions, appetites and propensities calculated ... to render them useful to each other in their social connections"[6]—if only to win the love and esteem that gratify the self.

Along with the right of man to be free and independent, the Founders asserted a strong belief that man was most magnanimous when functioning as a free individual. Jefferson for his part argued that men have an instinctive moral sense that compels them to respond with assistance when their neighbors are in distress.[7] In examining the scientific evidence to test Jefferson's contention, James Q. Wilson found ample evidence that individuals do have a "moral sense" and that it is formed out of their earliest interactions in the family. Scholarly studies of altruism, for example, demonstrate that the general pattern of warm familial relationships is striking. In a study of Christians who rescued Jews during the Holocaust, the long-term rescuers were very close to their parents, one or both of whom held strong moral convictions. The same pattern reappears in a study of people who were active for long periods in the civil rights movement during the 1960s. Compared to those who were only briefly involved, the fully committed activists had a warm and close relationship with one or both parents.[8]

By fostering human relationships of a type not always found in the wider society, the family fulfills an indispensable social function. As the Pope wrote in *Familiaris Consortio:*

The relationships between members of the family community are inspired and guided by the law of "free giving." By respecting and fostering personal dignity in each and every one as the only basis for value, this free giving takes the form of heartfelt acceptance, encounter and dialogue, disinterested availability, generous service and deep solidarity.[9]

In reviewing a wide variety of studies in developmental psychology, Wilson found that generous children were indeed raised by parents who offered nurturing love and consistent discipline and who themselves engaged in helping others. Rather than caring intensely only for members of the immediate family, children and adults who experienced love at home were precisely the people who were most likely to aid perfect strangers, often at risk to themselves.[10]

The empirical evidence, then, provides a powerful rebuttal to the conception of the moral agent as an abstract force, stripped of the intimacy and particularity of the family ties that undergird moral experience in everyday life. Michael Novak argues that moral realism itself is the one habit learned in the family that is most essential for successful self-government:

> [F]amily life is no utopia. It isn't meant to be. Its purpose is to instruct us in the painful but also mind-enlarging angularities of human nature. Such realism, vital to any free republic, arises from having your own self-images punctured, from learning to endure tragedies together, from penetrating one another's weaknesses, and from learning to forgive, to love, to be tolerant, and to support. Without such learning how could any civil society survive?[11]

In order to have meaningful content, love for humanity, for the stranger on the street corner, must evolve from the privilege of basic human affections—the experience of one heart knowing another.

While grounded in moral realism, acts of personal kindness elevate and ennoble the doer from within, and, in learning the unique worth of love, theologian Walter Rauschenbusch observed, we learn to feel the worth of those we ought to love.[12] Thus, love undergirds both moral autonomy and a sense of the dignity that belongs to every individual. Political coercion, by contrast, is a flimsy tool for social cohesion. "The frequency with which our communities have to fall back on ... coercion is a symptom of the failure of love, for love can usually dispense with force. The more love, the less force; the more force, the less love,"[13] Rauschenbusch wrote.

To the extent that centralized government usurps the space in which families and neighbors thrive—and thereby politicizes all relationships—it trumpets reductionist individualism and denies the power of love. Collectivism makes its mistake in assuming that virtues like selflessness and generosity are a part of human nature. Asserting that man has a moral sense (or a variation on self-interest that mimics a moral sense) is not to say that man is inherently virtuous or altruistic. If men were angels, the loss of family would exact no price.

A Revival of Community

It is also true, however, that strong families require strong communities. Charles Murray explains "affiliation is a means whereby people of common values are enabled to enact those values."[14] A functioning community that promotes a wide array of affiliations provides an extremely important venue both for practicing virtue and for passing down to the next generation the habit of virtue. The passing of values from parent to child, in fact, presupposes outlets for practice because it involves—as Murray puts it—a "reality test."

> How does one bequeath a habit of helping others, of giving, of generosity, if this has not been a part of one's own life? ...

> Watching parents support compassionate politicians just isn't
> the same. … If parents are engaged in directly paying other
> people in the community—supporting local institutions—
> they at least must do such things as choose whom they will
> pay and how much. And even these actions provide a richer
> basis for instruction than signing a 1040 Form and then try-
> ing to explain compassion to the child in the abstract.[15]

Wilson's empirical findings concur: generous children are in fact the sons and daughters of generous parents. He also discovers, however, that human sympathy is fragile. Behavior depends, not only on the development of right instinct, but on the extent to which the circumstances create a sense of personal responsibility. Adam Smith devised a famous thought experiment to demonstrate the point: If a man were to learn of the destruction of 100 million Chinese, he might lament their passing, but in a moment would return placidly to his business or leisure. But we would recoil at the thought of a man who in order to save his little finger would will the death of the very same number of distant Chinese. "If our sentiments were directed simply by our love of humanity," Wilson observes, "we might feel equal anguish at both tragedies, but we do not."[16] Adam Smith provides the explanation:

> When the happiness or misery of others depends in any
> respect upon our conduct, we dare not, as self-love might
> suggest to us, prefer the interest of one to that of many. The
> man within immediately calls.[17]

Conversely, when the happiness or misery of others bears no relation to our conduct, the man within remains silent.

Given the evidence that there is a "man within," the more appropriate question is—not whether human beings are capable of strong community—but why do we not see more evidence of community already in play.[18] The answer reflects Adam Smith's insight about human nature, for civil institutions by definition are groupings of flesh-and-blood men. To the extent that the welfare state has eliminated the necessity of a father who provides, it has reduced the sense of personal responsibility that kept him at home through good times and bad. To the extent that Washington hires social workers to do the job instead, Sioux City will almost certainly experience a decline in the numbers of men and women who feel compelled to volunteer their time at the end of a long day. In the words of Nathan Glazer, the reason social policy weakens civil institutions is:

> the simple reality that every piece of social policy substitutes for some traditional arrangement, whether good or bad, a new arrangement in which public authorities take over, at least in part, the role of the family, of the ethnic and neighborhood group, of the voluntary associations.[19]

In Marvin Olasky's turn of phrase, bad charity drives out good.

A Revival of Faith

When families no longer have the benefit of strong communities—and many children no longer even have the benefit of family—reviving civil society is admittedly more complex than merely relimiting the size of the welfare state. Pulling out the knife, as Professor DiIulio says, is unlikely to resuscitate the dying man.[20] But neither will a fresh stab wound do the trick. Civil society must derive its strength from non-political sources, and in all probability those sources must spring from a revival of religious faith. Relimiting government is essential precisely because government can stultify, but never revivify, religion.

When public order is lost and the center does not hold, fidelity to truth demands at least weighing the evidence that faith-based drug addiction programs save more lives than their secular counterparts.[21] Short of rigorous empirical calculations, fidelity to the truth demands engaging in a simple thought experiment: "If you are walking down the street in urban America and see four formidable-looking young males approaching, would you relax a little if you knew they had just emerged from a Bible study?" Probably, yes. The federal government's own surveys of the professional literature confirm that attachment to church is inversely related to violence.[22] Given the scale of the current crisis and the clarity of the evidence in defense of faith, many secular authorities are willing to give religion its due. The danger is not simply that government will soften its bias against faith-based programs too late, but even that government dollars will disarm the very emphasis on faith that made those programs a success in the first place.

Government contracting with community-based institutions, including religious institutions, will almost certainly result in a more efficient and effective delivery of services. The issue at hand, however, is neither efficiency nor material quality. The issue is transforming lives ravaged, not by a lack of material resources, but by a lack of the spiritual and moral fiber necessary to sustain independence. In a comprehensive study of religious charities, Amy Sherman concludes:

> The most effective groups challenge those who embrace faith to live out its moral implications in every significant area of their lives, from breaking drug addictions and repairing family relationships to recommitting themselves to the value of honest work. But state social-service contracts aren't necessarily concerned with such outcomes; they focus on meals served, beds available, and checks cashed.[23]

Faith-based programs, like men, cannot serve both God and mammon.

Even programs that retain their original vision are likely to face burdensome regulations that dilute the emphasis on faith. In explaining why faith-based programs succeed when state-licensed versions fail, Ed MacClellan, executive director of the Florida Association of Christian Child Caring Agencies (FACC-CA) summarizes his experience in plain, unvarnished English: "'In the licensed homes you'll find Jesus, but you'll have to look for Him. He's put away in the chapel or in a closet. … Go to one of our homes, and Jesus is gonna open the front door. That's the difference.'"[24] Regardless of right or wrong, the fact is that Jesus is unlikely to be opening the door at a public housing project any time soon. Faith-minded policy makers must accept that limitation for the present, and plan accordingly.

While the loss of a programmatic emphasis on religion is the most obvious compromise, government funding also changes the quality of personal relationships in subtle ways that can undercut any remaining vestiges of faith. Government paperwork diverts time from the face-to-face ministry that is the single most important corrective to the bureaucratic model—and the most likely avenue to spiritual renewal. Quite often the very thing needed, says Virgil Gulker, founder of Kids Hope USA, is simply "a person who cares, befriending another person who is lonely."[25] Star Parker, former welfare recipient, says from personal experience that the question posed to welfare recipients must be: "God or government?"[26] Government money damages the credibility of the personal example individual volunteers can set for the beneficiaries of their programs. Reverend Eddie Edwards, who oversees a community development organization in east Detroit called Joy of Jesus, explains: "When we are working with people in the community, helping them become self-sufficient, helping them get off welfare, it would be extremely difficult to tell them to get off welfare if we were on some kind of public assistance."[27] Indeed, the most powerful witness men and women of faith can offer is that dependence on God obviates the need for dependence on the state.

As long as state funding remains a part of the landscape, the church may do good works, but it will fail to realize its full potential as the vital center of community life. The heart of Charles Murray's argument about the prospects for a rebirth of civil society must be applied with particular urgency to the institution that is charged with remoralizing civil society. "The church will be a satisfying institution of community life (not just religious life) to the extent that the members have something important to do"—that will not otherwise be done. But "that institutional role will atrophy to the extent that it does not."[28] Just as it will be impossible to secure the benefits of community on the cheap, it will prove impossible to restore the influence of faith in America without churchgoers paying a rather steep price to vindicate that faith in their own lives, day by day.

Lest the burden seem too overwhelming, Virgil Gulker places the problem in perspective: "Somehow the statistics cover up the fact that behind every number is a name and a face—a real person with a real need. Categories and percentages seem beyond our grasp, but individuals can be helped."[29] Faith believes that the power of just one changed life is in fact more powerful than an activist state.

Ultimately, collectivism itself is at war with faith, for it is a vision not of individuals finding love and renewal in the presence of God, but of godlike individuals contriving the salvation of the masses. To vindicate the exaltation of an elite—often in the face of demonstrated failures to deliver the promised goods—collectivism insists upon an abstraction called "society" to which all moral problems finally refer. By absolving individuals of personal responsibility, collectivism enervates the faith that springs from man's reckoning with his own inadequacy. But it also leaves real, flesh-and-blood individuals hurting, by decreasing the likelihood that men will stir themselves to serve each other at the deepest point of need. As Mr. Goodman lamented of Mr. Fantom, "Between the great thing [man] cannot do, and the little one that he will not do, life passes, and nothing will be done."

What Can Be Done?

In short, a myriad of the "little things" that together will equal more than the sum of the parts. In 1976, Dr. Virgil Gulker founded an organization called LOVE, INC that seeks to bridge the gap between needy individuals and suburban church members. Someone once observed that LOVE, INC is distinctive because it has no heroes. Its sole purpose is to mobilize ordinary individuals to serve the poor, by making the needs both specific and manageable and by providing the appropriate training for volunteers. Today, some 4,000 churches nationwide are involved in LOVE, INC, while other individuals like Reverend Ronald Moore in Jackson, Mississippi, are developing their own training curriculum to help mobilize a critical mass of churches.

Dr. Gulker, for his part, has launched a new venture called Kids Hope USA that links adult volunteers in one-to-one relationships with at-risk children. Echoing Wilson's empirical findings, Dr. Gulker speaks from experience: "[When] suffering people remain nameless and faceless, a mass 'out there' who do not activate our sense of personal responsibility, ... [w]hen we lack direct contact with people's pain, their needs become merely one item on our agenda—and not necessarily an important item. ... Thus ministry shaped by distance ... is fatal to those in need."[30] Ministry to individuals one by one, on the other hand, is life-giving. Americans have grown too accustomed to sweeping government action, aimed at amorphous collective masses. We must learn to see social problems as individual responsibilities, but first we must affix names and faces to the need.

Secondly, we must find ways to divert economic resources from failed government programs to successful private-sector initiatives. But a word of caution at the outset.

Welfare state advocates often defend bureaucratic programs by arguing that the private sector cannot possibly replicate existing levels of government spending. "Based on the current welfare model," Father Robert Sirico replies, "they are right. All levels of government spend $950 billion a year on welfare programs. Charities, excluding churches, spend less than half this sum (about $360 billion). Private efforts clearly cannot assume the functions of the present welfare state. But why should they? An annual welfare budget of $300 billion is roughly three times the amount of money it would take to raise the incomes of all poor people above the poverty line."[31]

The welfare delivery system, like any other bureaucracy-laden government monopoly, is woefully inefficient. One study found that less than 35 cents out of every welfare dollar was paid in cash directly to the needy.[32] Every year, welfare consumes more tax dollars without any incentives to cut costs or monitor results. In the words of Indianapolis Mayor Steve Goldsmith, "The federal government offers the best deal in town: The more you spend, the more you get. Don't worry about results."[33] The national average spending for government-subsidized homeless shelters is $22 per person per day. By contrast, Sister Connie Driscoll operates St. Martin de Porres House of Hope, a homeless shelter in Chicago, at an average cost of $6.73 per person per day. Sister Connie receives no government funding. She does get results. The House of Hope has the most impressive success rate in Chicago. Only 6 percent of its residents find themselves on the street again.

The key to success, of course, is that Sister Connie sets behavioral standards for the receipt of assistance. The changes in behavior pose savings over and above the dollars saved by a more efficient delivery of goods and services. In a monograph titled "The Market Foundations of Philanthropy," Richard McKenzie explains:

> The donors' demands for reforms on the part of recipients carry weight for a simple reason: the recipients understand that the private aid can be withdrawn (without an act of Congress), which means that private aid is much more likely to be performance-based and cost-effective.[34]

Just as government bureaucrats treat the agency budget as a proxy goal to be maximized, recipients of open-ended checks face their own perverse incentives to perpetuate the very behavior that drains the tax dollars of millions of hard-working Americans year after year. The tax burden in turn undermines the economic expansiveness that could create jobs—and fund additional philanthropic giving.[35]

Just as the private sector need not replace the welfare state dollar for dollar, efforts to build private sector capacity do not depend on an increase in charitable giving by every American. Only a reasonable percentage of the population must participate, and voluntary giving is certainly an attractive alternative to taxation. Far from serving as an efficient way to raise money for public purposes, taxation hurts the economy by creating a disincentive effect for production as well as a new layer of compliance costs. Both costs disappear under a voluntary system. Until the 20th-century love affair with government, James Payne notes in *The Public Interest,* logic dictated that voluntarism was the "principal way money was raised for social purposes."[36]

Despite the growing bite of government taxation, recent levels of charitable giving remain impressive. If the value of volunteer labor is included, the current value of private charity exceeds all government welfare spending combined.[37] Payne concludes:

> [Academic preoccupation with the free-rider problem] overlooks the complexity of human behavior. Human beings can be generous as well as selfish, and this generosity makes possible the hundreds of thousands of voluntary giving arrangements that we see all across the country. ... The moral power of this kind of voluntary transaction can never be achieved with a tax system based on force. ... It is worth speculating how such giving might thrive in a society that decided to emphasize it, in a society where children were taught, from their earliest days, that voluntary giving is needed to sustain civilization.[38]

Charitable activity does appear to correlate closely with a coherent system of beliefs. *The American Enterprise* reports that government-shrinking conservatives are more than twice as likely to volunteer time and likely to give more than twice as big a percentage of their annual incomes to charity. The most generous subgroup within the population is religious conservatives.[39]

Research shows, moreover, that giving patterns among individual Americans have changed along with changes in the role of government. From the early 1940s through 1964, as the U.S. grew wealthier, an increasing portion of wealth was given to charities. In the mid-1960s, however, the trend was reversed—despite the fact that total wealth continued to increase. A rise in charitable giving did not reappear until 1981 (during a period of hard times, incidentally) when the Reagan Administration proposed cuts in social welfare spending and urged a return to voluntarism.[40] Richard McKenzie has demonstrated that, as a result, charitable giving by Americans in the 1980s increased by all possible measures,[41] while voluntarism made a resurgence among both college students and professionals. In 1979, about 300 companies had programs to encourage workers to participate in community service projects. By the late 1980s, the number had increased to 600, and at least 200 companies were sending workers into the community on company time. Between 1984 and 1989, the number of Americans reporting charitable volunteer work in Gallup polls rose from 34 percent to 50 percent.[42]

Anecdotal evidence from more recent experiments also indicates that private giving increases in response to cuts in public funding. In reaction to a Wisconsin Supreme Court injunction against Milwaukee's expanded school-choice program, which allows parents to use vouchers at private sectarian schools, residents throughout the state donated more than $1.2 million to help children stay in the schools of their choice.[43] The Public Broadcasting Service reports a 12 percent increase in private giving over last year. Federal funds for PBS are scheduled to decrease 6 percent in 1996 and more in 1997. According to Stu Kantor, PBS associate director of corporate information, "I think people have been responding to reports in the news about budgetary pressures facing PBS."[44]

A number of technical analyses confirm, conversely, that government spending crowds out private philanthropy. Russell Roberts, for example, concluded succinctly in the *Journal of Political Economy:* "Current data and evidence from the Depression yield support for the crowding-out result. The huge growth in public transfers in the 1930s crowded out private antipoverty efforts and fundamentally changed the nature of private charity. Current data also support this conclusion."[45] The explanation rests on a simple truth about human nature: People tend to defer responsibility when someone else will answer the bell. Charles Murray captures the problem with characteristic genius:

> At the microlevel, the dialogue between the government and the citizen goes roughly like this:
> Do you want to go out and feed the hungry or are you going to sit here and watch television?
> I'm tired. What'll happen if I don't go?
> Well, if you don't go I guess I'll just have to do it myself.
> In that case, you go.[46]

By rewriting the dialogue between citizen and government, cuts in government spending alone are likely to trigger increases in voluntary giving. At the very least, taxpayers should be allowed to shift a percentage of their personal income tax payments from public programs to private charities. Several legislators have already proposed a dollar-for-dollar tax credit for contributions to charities engaged in poverty-fighting efforts (defined by the income level of the service recipients). Ideally, taxpayers would be allowed to divert up to 41 percent of their personal income tax payments—that is, the share of total individual income taxes that currently goes to federal means-tested welfare programs.[47] For each tax dollar allocated to private sector charity, public sector charity would be reduced by a dollar. Thus, with the credit, private organizations would at last be able to compete on a level playing field for welfare tax dollars. Taxpayers would have the opportunity to indicate their preference: more government bureaucracy or individuals helping individuals down the street?

The dollars sent to poverty-fighting organizations would not undermine giving to museums and symphony orchestras because money donated to cultural institutions would still be tax-deductible. At present, the tax code permits charitable deductions from taxable income—not from the check owed the I.R.S. Thus, under the current system, donors in higher tax brackets benefit more from charitable giving. Congress should consider elevating the charitable deduction to 120 percent, but also restoring the deduction to non-itemizers.

Approximately seven out of 10 taxpayers opt for the standard deduction—even when they have donated substantial amounts—usually because they have no mortgage interest deduction. An above-the-line deduction for charitable contributions for non-itemizing taxpayers would not only benefit many middle-to-low-income people, but it is also likely to increase charitable giving to an array of neighborhood organizations involved in poverty prevention efforts. During 1985-1986, when a charitable deduction for non-itemizers was last in place, charitable giving among non-itemizers did in fact rise dramatically. Tax provisions that empower *everyone,* not just people of means, are precisely the reforms most likely to benefit the health clinics and mentoring programs in low- and middle-income neighborhoods. Surveys show that people who make the least are inclined to give the highest percentage of their income to help neighbors in need.[48]

While block grants simply reallocate power among public bureaucracies, tax breaks for giving restore power to individual citizens and communities—power that in turn will fuel the ethic of caring that is the true hallmark of freedom. In *Prospects for Conservatives,* Russell Kirk wrote: "The enlightened conservative ... knows that the just and ordered society is that in which Love governs us, so far as Love ever can reign in this world of sorrows; and he knows that the anarchical or the tyrannical society is that in which Love lies corrupt."[49]

Love lies corrupted today by a welfare state that asks men to love not individuals, but faceless collectivities. If Kirk is correct that men are "put into this world ... to aspire toward the triumph of Love,"[50] then we must aspire toward the end of a system that thrusts our benevolence out to the remotest periphery, to people whose names and faces we do not know and whose hands we cannot hold. Life for them will not be whole again until we learn to love, one heart at a time.

—*Jennifer E. Marshall*

Reprinted from *Family Policy,* published six times a year by Family Research Council. Annual subscriptions are available for $15. *Contact:* Family Research Council, 801 G Street, N.W., Washington, D.C. 20001. *Phone:* 1-800-225-4008. *President:* Gary L. Bauer; *Editor:* William R. Mattox, Jr.; *Editorial and Production Support:* Anne Redd, Rosanne Dupras, Deanna Carlson, Charles A. Donovan, Valerie Stambaugh; *Distribution:* Kevin Gilliam, Steve McIntyre. Vol. 8, Number 6; Copyright December 1995 by Family Research Council. All rights reserved.

ENDNOTES

1 Meyer, Frank S., *In Defense of Freedom: A Conservative Credo.* (Chicago: University of Chicago Press, 1962) p. 128.

2 *Ibid.,* pp. 87-88.

3 Michael S. Joyce, "Saving Philanthropy from Itself," *First Things,* February 1995, no. 50, p. 50.

4 F. A. Hayek, "The Moral Element in Free Enterprise," *The Spiritual and Moral Significance of Free Enterprise,* New York: National Association of Manufacturers, pp. 26-27, quoted in Father Robert A. Sirico, CSP, *A Moral Basis for Liberty,* London: Institute of Economic Affairs Health and Welfare Unit, 1994, p. 7.

5 Alexis de Tocqueville, *Democracy in America,* ed. J. P. Mayer, trans. George Lawrence, New York: Doubleday, 1969, p. 62, quoted in Charles Murray, *In Pursuit of Happiness and Good Government,* San Francisco: Institute for Contemporary Studies, 1994, p. xii.

6 John Adams, Discourses on Davila, quoted in Charles Murray, *In Pursuit of Happiness and Good Government,* San Francisco: Institute for Contemporary Studies, 1994, p. 131.

7 Murray, Charles, *In Pursuit of Happiness and Good Government.* San Francisco: Institute for Contemporary Studies, 1994, pp. 129-130.

8 Wilson, James Q., *The Moral Sense.* New York: The Free Press, 1993, pp. 38-39.

9 Pope John Paul II, *Familiaris Consortio,* p. 43, quoted in David Wagner, "The Family and American Constitutional Law," Family Research Council, 1994, p. 8.

10 Wilson, *op. cit.,* pp. 45, 47.

11 Michael Novak, "The Family: Thumbs Up!" (undated copy obtained from office of author).

12 Rauschenbusch, Walter. *Dare We Be Christians?* (Cleveland, Ohio: The Pilgrim Press, 1914) p. 3.

13 *Ibid.,* pp. 32-33.

14 Murray, *op. cit.,* p. 216.

15 *Ibid.,* pp. 236-237.

16 Wilson, *op. cit.,* pp. 50-51.

17 Adam Smith, *The Theory of Moral Sentiments,* III.3.4, p. 136, quoted in Charles Murray, *In Pursuit of Happiness and Good Government,* pp. 239-240.

18 I am indebted to Charles Murray for framing this central question in *In Pursuit of Happiness and Good Government,* p. 224.

19 Glazer, Nathan, *The Limits of Social Policy.* (Cambridge, Massachusetts: Harvard University Press, 1988) p. 7.

[20] See, for example, John J. DiIulio, "The Coming of the Super-Predators," *The Weekly Standard,* November 27, 1995, vol. 1, no. 11, p. 27.

[21] Amy Sherman reports that Christian-based substance-abuse recovery programs boast as much as a 70 to 80 percent success rate, while secular therapeutic programs report an average success rate of 6 to 10 percent. See Amy L. Sherman, "Cross Purposes: Will Conservative Welfare Reform Corrupt Religious Charities?" *Policy Review,* Fall 1995, no. 74, p. 58.

[22] See Patrick F. Fagan, "The Real Root Causes of Violent Crime: The Breakdown of Marriage, Family, and Community," *The Heritage Foundation Backgrounder,* March 17, 1995, no. 1026, pp. 29-30, for a comprehensive review of the professional literature. In "The Coming of the Super-Predators" (*The Weekly Standard,* November 27, 1995), John DiIulio cites a 1986 study by Harvard economist Richard Freeman and a study by a panel of leading specialists just published in the journal *Criminology*—both of which confirm that, while much work remains to be done, there is substantial empirical evidence that religion serves as an insulator against crime and delinquency.

[23] Sherman, *op. cit.*

[24] Frederica Mathewes-Green, "Their Ship Has Come In," *World,* September 23, 1995, vol. 10, no. 18, p. 15.

[25] Gulker, Virgil with Ken Wilson. *Helping You Is Helping Me: How a New Breed of Volunteers Can Make a Difference.* (Ann Arbor, Michigan: Servant Publications, 1993) p. 43.

[26] Star Parker, Address to the Christian Coalition Road to Victory Conference, Washington, D.C., September 8, 1995.

[27] Sherman, *op. cit.,* p. 60.

[28] Murray, *op. cit.,* p. 228.

[29] Gulker, *op. cit.,* p. 44.

[30] Gulker, Virgil with Kevin Perrotta. *Help Is Just Around the Corner: How Love Inc. Mobilizes Care for the Need.* (Lake Mary, Florida: Creation House, 1988) pp. 33-34.

[31] Father Robert A. Sirico, "Terms of the Welfare Debate," *The Washington Times,* April 19, 1995.

[32] Cited in Pete du Pont and Jeffrey Eisenach, "Poor Substitute," *National Review,* December 31, 1994, vol. 46, no. 25, p. 51.

[33] Quoted in testimony by Congressman Joe Knollenberg before the House Ways and Means Committee Subcommittee on Human Resources, January 30, 1995.

[34] Richard B. McKenzie, "The Market Foundations of Philanthropy," The Philanthropy Roundtable, 1994, p. 25.

[35] The link between economic growth and philanthropy is well-established. See, for example, Richard McKenzie, "The Market Foundations of Philanthropy," The Philanthropy Roundtable, 1994, p. 9.

[36] James L. Payne, "The End of Taxation?" *The Public Interest,* Summer 1993, no. 112, p. 113.

[37] John C. Goodman, Gerald W. Reed, Peter J. Ferrara, "Why Not Abolish the Welfare State?," National Center for Policy Analysis Policy Report No. 187, October 1994, p. 23.

[38] Payne, James L., *op. cit.*, pp. 114, 117-118.

[39] *The American Enterprise,* March/April 1995, vol. 6, no. 2, p. 19.

[40] Charles Murray, "How Government Has Hurt Philanthropy," *Philanthropy,* November/December 1988.

[41] Richard B. McKenzie, *Was the Decade of the 1980s a "Decade of Greed"?* St. Louis: Center for the Study of American Business.

[42] "The New Volunteerism," *Newsweek,* February 8, 1988, pp. 42-43, and "Special Report: The New Volunteers," *Newsweek,* July 10, 1989, pp. 36-66.

[43] Reported in *The Washington Times,* September 6, 1995.

[44] Cited in *Alternatives in Philanthropy,* Capital Research Center, November 1995, p. 9.

[45] Russell D. Roberts, "A Positive Model of Private Charity and Public Transfers," *Journal of Political Economy,* 1984, vol. 92, no. 1, p. 147.

[46] Murray, *In Pursuit of Happiness and Good Government, op. cit.,* p. 225.

[47] Goodman, Reed, and Ferrara, *op. cit.,* p. 30.

[48] Cited in Pete du Pont and Jeffrey Eisenach, "Poor Substitute," *National Review,* December 31, 1994, vol. 46, no. 25, p. 51.

[49] Kirk, Russell, *Prospects for Conservatives.* (Washington, D.C.: Regnery Gateway, 1989) p. 21.

[50] *Ibid.*

APPENDIX II

THE LAST WORD

MY FAVORITE VOLUNTEER

In all the years of working with church members, my favorite volunteer is a woman in her mid-60s. For a long time, whenever I would speak with her, she would talk about friends who had died and about her arthritis.

She also talked wistfully about a great disappointment in her life. As a girl she had set her goal to become a teacher. But she came from a poor family, and after the eighth grade she was required to go out to work to help support her family. Later she married, and then she sometimes had to work outside the home to supplement her husband's earnings and sometimes stayed at home and cared for her four children. She never regretted any of this, but she wondered what might have been.

I approached this woman one day and said that we needed tutors for Hispanic and Oriental children. "Will you tutor?" I asked. In effect, I was asking, "Will you become the teacher you always wanted to be?"

"I can't," she replied. "I'm too old."

"You're not too old," I replied.

"I don't have the skills," she objected.

"I'll train you," I said.

She finally agreed to go through the training program—probably to get me off her back. But she told me she wasn't planning to tutor; she would just help in other ways. "Fine," I said.

At the end of the training, I asked her to tutor two Hispanic boys. She gave in.

In subsequent months, when I saw her, I would ask, "How is your arthritis?"

"What?" she would say. Instead, she would tell me about the boys.

"Have you been reading the obituaries lately?" I would ask.

"No," she would answer, and then tell me about the problems the boys were having. The boys became her life.

A week before Christmas she was sitting in her living room, and she heard a terrible commotion outside. When she opened the front door, there stood the two boys in the snow. They had brought all their classmates to sing Christmas carols to their "favorite teacher."

It is hard to imagine that anyone anywhere was happier that night. She had become the teacher she had wanted to be.

I often think that this woman, who is my mother, is like many other people: all reticence and excuses, but when they get the right opportunity, the training and the encouragement, they succeed.

—*Virgil Gulker*
Director, Kids Hope USA